FUTURESCAN

Health Care Trends and Implications

2024

T0292940

Balancing New Imperatives for a Changing Environment

Ian Morrison, PhD

The health care environment is continuing to transform as the need for greater health equity, the rapid deployment of new technology, and workforce shortages impact the operations of hospitals and health systems. As these developments converge under the specter of climate change and the economic realities of funding care for marginalized populations, health care executives have complicated and challenging decisions to make that need careful consideration in the context of their organizations' missions.

In this edition of *Futurescan*, we hear from eight subject matter experts who are at the forefront of new approaches to the advancement of health care in this country. They cover such diverse topics as the growing Medicaid population and the social determinants of health that impact patients' well-being, sustainability strategies to mitigate climate change and its effects, the use of technology to lower the cost of care and move it into patients' homes, and the redesign of work to meet the changing demands of our shrinking health care workforce. To frame these articles, an expert in health care finance sets the tone for our current economic reality and the role government plays in our future sustainability.

Health care leaders who are looking ahead and strategizing about how their organizations can survive and even thrive over the next five years will learn much from these experts and their recommendations for balancing new imperatives in a changing environment.

Redesigning Work While Meeting the Demands of the Workforce

Workforce issues remain the number-one concern of hospital and health system CEOs across the United States, and staffing shortages are the primary reason why. Joanne M. Conroy, MD, CEO and president of Dartmouth Health, delineates possible solutions for health care leaders to consider when trying to stabilize their workforce.

Without the required number of personnel at all levels, Conroy believes health care leaders need to redesign workflows that provide quality patient care while attracting and retaining new talent. Like many health systems responding to the pandemic, Dartmouth Health moved most non–patient

About the Subject Matter Expert

Ian Morrison, PhD, is an author, consultant, and futurist. He received an undergraduate degree from the University of Edinburgh, Scotland; a graduate degree from the University of Newcastle upon Tyne, England; and an interdisciplinary doctorate in urban studies from the University of British Columbia, Canada. He is the author of several books, including the best-selling *The Second Curve: Managing the Velocity of Change.* Morrison is the former president of the Institute for the Future and a founding partner of Strategic Health Perspectives, a forecasting service for clients in the health care industry.

care positions to be fully remote in 2020, an arrangement that has been welcomed by many employees. Conroy suggests reworking the patient care model in several ways, such as having nurses operate at the top of their licenses so that they can supervise other trained staff. Dartmouth Health has also been creating its own employee pipelines by training pharmacy technicians, surgical techs, medical assistants, and phlebotomists. Technology can be used to supplant or support workforces and care processes, and many innovative health systems are devoting considerable resources to delivering a digital experience, which could also reduce the need for certain workers.

Conroy urges health care executives to balance these strategies in ways that meet the needs of their current workforce. She recommends that executives consider how to engage employees to be part of their workforce rather than forcing them to fit into an inflexible model of work.

Care in the Home

Medical care delivered in the home is nothing new, but the COVID-19 pandemic highlighted how effective hospital-level care could be when delivered in a home setting. Scott Rissmiller, MD, executive vice president and chief physician executive at Atrium Health, presents a compelling case for hospital-at-home care that health care leaders would do well to consider. During COVID, rather than admitting patients, Atrium developed protocols and clinical pathways to safely and successfully care for COVID patients in their homes. The initiative proved so successful that Atrium Health now treats a wide variety of conditions with its hospital-at-home program.

Hundreds of organizations throughout the country have received funding from the Centers for Medicare & Medicaid Services to help them provide extensive hospital-at-home services. The resulting effects of lowered costs, greater patient satisfaction, and enhanced outcomes have fueled a growing trend to create hospital-at-home programs at hospitals and health systems across the

country. They are becoming an innovative way to expand access, address health inequities, control costs, and improve the patient experience.

Sustainability Strategies

Climate change is having a major impact on the livability of communities throughout the world. In this country, health care accounts for 8.5 percent of all emissions. Rod Hochman, MD, president and CEO of Providence Health, offers tactics that can substantially lower this carbon footprint. Providence has committed to being carbon-negative by 2030 and was one of the first health systems to sign the voluntary White House/HHS Health Sector Climate Pledge to cut 50 percent of greenhouse gas generation by 2030.

A reduction in energy consumption can be achieved by the installation of LED lighting and automated building systems and the updating or replacing of heavy equipment to maximize efficiency. Remote work can result in using fewer resources per capita, per square foot, and per employee. The use of anesthesia with lower emissions can have a significant effect on the emission of greenhouse gases. New methods of recycling can reduce the amount of waste that makes its way into landfills.

Hochman stresses that patients are being impacted by climate change, which disproportionately affects people at the lower end of the socioeconomic spectrum. Climate change is directly related to health and health equity. Ultimately, health care executives have a societal and moral obligation to try to minimize the diseases and conditions that stem from our changing climate.

The Future of Population and Public Health

In an article that continues the theme of addressing population health and health equity, Omar Lateef, DO, president and chief executive officer (CEO) of RUSH, and David A. Ansell, MD, RUSH's senior vice president for community health equity, discuss strategies for ensuring that medical needs are addressed equitably at both an individual and a community level. Lateef and Ansell maintain that racial health inequity is a public health crisis in the United States. They believe that community-based and public health initiatives should be key components of any plan to address health disparities in marginalized communities. Health systems—often the largest employers in their communities—have the ability to stimulate economic growth locally via anchor strategies.

According to Ansell, the pandemic highlighted the need to create closer hospital partnerships with public health departments and community organizations. Forward-thinking health care executives are going beyond community health assessments to advocate for public health funding to create infrastructure projects, such as a public–private system to build and maintain labs and a shared information-technology infrastructure for advancing joint initiatives that promote population health. Health care executives can have the biggest effect on the future of population and public health by eliminating health inequities and the root causes that contribute to them: poverty and systemic racism.

Direct Contracting with Employers

Self-insured employers, frustrated with the cost and complexity of traditional health insurance contracts, are bypassing insurance companies to establish direct-to-employer contracts with local health systems. For health systems, this growing trend presents an opportunity to embrace direct contracting; however, a successful relationship can be challenging to implement and comes with risks. Jane Thornhill, MSA, vice president of business operations at the Henry Ford Physician Network, shares lessons learned about making these relationships as mutually beneficial as possible.

For employers, a direct contract gives the employer tight control over the features and outcomes that are prioritized within a health plan. This can lead to cost savings and higher employee satisfaction and helps employers invest in their employees' health. Hospitals that are engaged in these direct-to-employer contracts will need to counsel employers to examine their health care claims data to understand which services are needed. It takes a dedicated team of people with specialized skills—often from the human resources department—to develop a direct contract.

The Economic Future of Health Care

Eric Jordahl, managing director at Kaufman, Hall & Associates, LLC, succinctly explains the effects of the national debt and its future risk to health care. The crux of the problem for hospitals and health systems is that the federal government's involvement in the US health care system is vast

and still growing, and there are many pressures on the government to reduce the costs of its involvement. Growth in government spending and thus the national debt is driven primarily by the federal government's major entitlement programs: Social Security, Medicare, and (shared with the states) Medicaid. Many health care organizations already receive more than 50 percent of their payments from Medicare and Medicaid. The federal government's entanglement in health care expenditures extends well beyond government payment programs, however: it also subsidizes significant portions of commercial health insurance expenditures through the tax-deductibility of private health insurance. The government thus has an interest not only in keeping Medicare and Medicaid expenditures under control but also in controlling the costs of commercial health insurance.

Aside from the pressures of government's vast influence over the finances of health care, hospitals and health systems also face economic challenges such as staffing shortages and the disruption of traditional care delivery models because of technology and innovation. An organization's balance sheet will be the essential bridge between the present and a future restructured health care sector. Given the many risks that hospitals and health systems face and the degree of uncertainty around some of the most

significant obstacles, Jordahl concludes that the journey is going to require very careful planning about how to size, position, and deploy liquidity, leverage, and investments.

Managing the Growing Medicaid Population

Nearly 150 million Americans rely on federal health care benefits through Medicare, Medicaid, and the State Children's Health Insurance Program. Over the next five years, hospitals and health systems can expect to see a dramatic increase in the number of patients who have Medicaid as their primary payment source and the number of individuals who are dual-eligible for both Medicare and Medicaid. In an article that stresses the importance of planning for the care provision of Medicaid patients over the next five years, Kameron Matthews, MD, JD, FAAFP, chief health officer at Cityblock Health, stresses the concept of "whole-person care" to adequately respond to these reimbursement and population trends. Patients who have experienced entrenched inequities have been marginalized for decades. Caring for the health of these individuals means addressing social and economic factors such as a person's financial stability, the home and neighborhood in which they live, their access to affordable health care, and their connection to community support.

Matthews asserts that the leading strategy to deliver whole-person care is the prioritization and expansion of primary care services. The tools for care teams should be adapted to reflect longitudinal and whole-person care across a person's life span, rather than reflecting the "point-in-time," episodic documentation seen in most current electronic health records. Technology and digital tools must improve hospitals' ability to meet the needs of these at-risk populations, allowing health systems to be as agnostic as possible toward a patient's form of insurance coverage. More comprehensive data on race, ethnicity, gender identity, and sexual orientation are also vital for addressing issues related to social determinants of health.

Responsible Innovation and the Digital Transformation of Health Care

According to Stephen Klasko, MD, executive-in-residence at General Catalyst, new digital solutions are bridging the gaps between providers and patients, transforming health care delivery. This metamorphosis is finally addressing health equity issues, especially in traditionally underserved communities. Over the next five years, hospitals and health care systems that begin to invest in and become involved with responsible innovation will be the drivers of change and supporters of health equity.

Responsible innovation refers to the development of ways to bring health care to underserved communities while keeping residents out of high-fixed-cost hospitals. Health leaders should consider collaborating with companies that provide services to nontraditional, overlooked, and underserved patient populations. Strategic health care executives who partner with emerging companies will be filling a critical need to create health assurance and health equity. Hospitals and health systems can benefit by codeveloping the innovations that they will use to care for disadvantaged populations. These innovations offer financial and technological rewards to health care organizations as well as improved health outcomes for the populations they serve. Klasko advises health care executives to work with their boards to identify ways to invest and diversify their portfolios, especially in digital innovations with a radical mindset.

Conclusion

The health care delivery system is already experiencing wholesale changes in how patients access care, who provides it, and where it is delivered. With growing fiscal pressures on government reimbursement, health care leaders would be well advised to heed Jordahl's recommendation to consider a structural "makeover" that aligns with health care's new economic probabilities and realities.

Redesigning Work While Meeting the Demands of the Workforce

with Joanne M. Conroy, MD, CEO and President of Dartmouth Health

Workforce issues remain the number-one concern of hospital and health system chief executive officers (CEOs) across the United States. "The world has changed since COVID in a couple of ways," says Joanne M. Conroy, MD, CEO and president of Dartmouth Health. Conroy has led New Hampshire's only academic health system since 2017, overseeing its expansion into Vermont through partnerships and collaborations. Burnout has caused many experienced clinicians to leave the field, and lower-level workers have left their positions for higher-paying jobs in other industries. "We simply don't have enough workers in the pipeline who will enable us to deliver care the way we've delivered it before," Conroy states. "We all need to think about how we can redesign our workflows so that we provide quality patient care while attracting and retaining new talent."

Conroy adds that most health care leaders are concerned with their organization's cost structure, with personnel being the largest expense. "I think most of us acknowledge that we were just getting by under previous reimbursement schedules, but the pandemic has shown us that it's unsustainable. We need to take a hard look at the costs involved in delivering health care and eliminate things that don't deliver value."

Like many health systems responding to the pandemic, Dartmouth Health moved most non–patient care positions to be fully remote in 2020. It is an arrangement that has been welcomed by many employees. "People really crave remote work and like to work at home at least a portion of the week," Conroy says, based on her system's experience during the pandemic and its aftermath. "We have found that it doesn't really interfere with productivity."

The Current Health Care Landscape

Dartmouth Health has devoted considerable resources to surveying and assessing its workforce. The findings indicate that there are other benefits of remote work beyond its appeal to employees.

About the Subject Matter Expert

Joanne M. Conroy, MD, has led Dartmouth Health as chief executive officer and president since 2017, overseeing the management of the state's only academic health system and largest private employer. The Dartmouth Health system includes four hospitals, a home health agency, and a long-standing relationship with the Geisel School of Medicine at Dartmouth to provide key academic and research collaborations and train the next generation of physicians. In December 2022, Conroy was ranked #18 on *Modern Healthcare*'s list of "100 Most Influential People in Healthcare." Other recent national and regional awards and honors of note include being named to *Becker's Hospital Review*'s "Top 113 Great Leaders in Healthcare" list and receiving the 2021 Citizen of the Year award from the *New Hampshire Union Leader*. Conroy was named to the American Hospital Association's (AHA's) board of trustees in 2019, and in 2022 she was named chair-elect designate to serve as chair of the AHA board in 2024.

"Our engagement surveys throughout the pandemic revealed one constant: that people who are fully remote are the most engaged and productive workforce," Conroy states. "Even hybrid workers are less engaged than fully remote workers. That surprised us."

Dartmouth Health leaders found that employees welcomed the autonomy to construct their days in ways that made them more professionally productive. Others preferred not having a lengthy commute. Based on extensive assessments, Dartmouth Health committed to making certain job categories fully and permanently remote. "Employees in those positions gave up their office space and received subsidies to work completely from home," says Conroy. "Between 25 and 30 percent of our workforce is now fully remote. We have workers in over 30 states, and the benefits outweigh the costs."

Moving hundreds of employees off campus had other positive outcomes besides accommodating employees who prefer remote work. "We liberated a lot of parking and office space that can be repurposed in other ways," Conroy states.

According to findings from the latest *Futurescan* survey, remote work is a trend that is here to stay. Fourteen percent of respondents said at least 75 percent of nonclinical business operations at their hospitals or health systems are currently performed off-site, remotely, or in a hybrid virtual work environment. The majority of health care leaders said it was likely or somewhat likely to be standard operating procedure by 2029.

The emerging economy of gig workers is another trend that is affecting hospitals and health systems. "These are employees who only want shift work, and we are not getting them for life," says Conroy. "They will be here for a year or two and then move on. It's up to us to find ways to connect them to the organization in a meaningful way while meeting their unique needs."

Strategies for Adapting to a Changing Workforce

What should C-suite executives evaluate as they look toward redesigning their

workforce strategy? "There has been a lot of deliberation on what job functions should be kept internally and what could be performed remotely, outsourced, or even moved offshore," Conroy says. "Functions that can be successful when fully remote include information technology, finance, most human resources work, call centers, and revenue cycle management."

The *Futurescan* survey showed a much smaller adoption of this strategy to date. Only five percent of CEOs say they have outsourced, offshored, or redesigned at least half of their organization's services. By 2029, however, 42 percent expect this transition of services to be likely or somewhat likely.

Many CEOs used to worry about jobs leaving the community they serve, but with low unemployment, this has not been such a concern. Conroy adds a caveat: "You can't really outsource a function that isn't working well. You must fix the process before sending it off-site." Functions that must be kept on-site at hospitals and health systems include direct patient care, support staff such as housekeeping and food services, security, the reception and information desk, and the supply chain that delivers medications and supplies.

While remote work is here to stay, challenges are inherent in the arrangement. Creating and maintaining an organizational culture is one concern. The loss of socialization and

collaboration for some employees is also a disadvantage. "Lateral problem-solving often happens in a groupthink setting," Conroy acknowledges. "We need to figure out how to do that with technology and other strategies. Some of our supervisors have set up Zoom meetings, dinners, happy hours, and departmental meetings every quarter to support team building and culture continuity." Dartmouth Health has also found a need to train supervisors on how to work with a remote workforce: "Team leaders have had to become more intentional in defining what makes employees productive. Our most successful supervisors are especially skilled in mentoring and creating a community."

Staff turnover presents a different set of challenges. In early 2022, 31 percent of hospitals reported a critical staffing shortage to the federal government (HealthData.gov 2020). A study released by the National Council of State Boards of Nursing (2023) reports that 100,000 registered nurses left the workforce during the past two years because of stress, burnout, and retirements. Another 610,388 reported an intent to leave by 2027. For most health systems, the shortage of workers at all levels requires that organizational leaders consider new staffing models.

Conroy suggests reevaluating the patient care model from several perspectives: "Can we have our nurses operate at the top of their licenses so that they

FUTURESCAN SURVEY RESULTS
Workforce

Health care executives from across the nation were asked how likely it is that the following will happen in their hospital or health system by 2029.

By 2029, at least 75 percent of nonclinical business operations at our hospital or health system will be performed off-site, remotely, or in a hybrid virtual work environment.

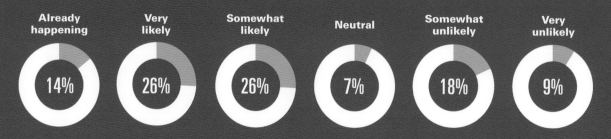

Already happening	Very likely	Somewhat likely	Neutral	Somewhat unlikely	Very unlikely
14%	26%	26%	7%	18%	9%

By 2029, 50 percent of our current hospital or health system shared services will be replaced with technology, off-shoring, outsourcing, or care redesign.

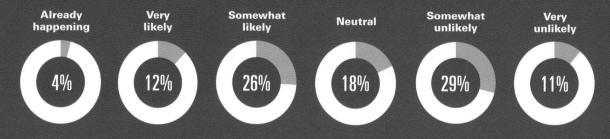

Already happening	Very likely	Somewhat likely	Neutral	Somewhat unlikely	Very unlikely
4%	12%	26%	18%	29%	11%

can supervise other trained staff, such as certified nursing assistants? That could result in a possible reduction in the need for nurses by 30 percent." Conroy proposes that a trained group of medical assistants in an operating room could perform the circulating component under the supervision of a registered nurse, who would manage a number of operating rooms.

These staffing models assume that employees with lower-level licenses are available, which has been a problem for smaller or rural communities. In response, Dartmouth Health has been creating its own employee pipelines through its Workforce Readiness Institute, which trains pharmacy technicians, surgical techs, medical assistants, and phlebotomists. "It takes about eight months to train surgical techs, and we pay them to learn during that time," says Conroy. "They are offered a job once they complete the coursework, and they go on to earn their certification."

Other health systems have also begun creating their own workforce of the future. Mary Washington Healthcare in Virginia partners with a local community college to offer an Earn While You Learn program for nursing students, with up to 60 learners each year. Freeman Health System in Missouri collaborated with a local college to provide education and employment for certified medical assistants through a 16-week paid apprentice program. Vanderbilt University Medical Center in Nashville, Tennessee, codeveloped a program to train current employees, including truck drivers and environmental services staff, to fill multiple medical assistant openings. During this training, workers receive their full salary plus tuition reimbursement.

Conroy says that some highly trained clinicians are conflicted when asked to work at the top of their license and supervise other employees. "We've heard some nurses say, 'I went into health care because I love my patients and want to work directly with them.' It's important to make these changes *with* nurses and not *to* them," she advises.

Where can technology be used to supplant or support workforces and care processes? "While you can't replace a vacancy with technology, you can use it to reduce the need for so many employees," Conroy notes. The new patient-care pavilion that Dartmouth Health has just completed includes a lift in each patient room that enables one nurse to move patients who previously would have required two or even four people to move. TV cameras also have been installed in every room so that a nurse can see the patient and conduct an assessment without actually being in the room.

MercyOne in Des Moines, Iowa, implemented a virtual nurse approach to staffing that uses two-way video-conferencing technology located in the patient's room. The virtual nurse assists bedside nurses in monitoring patients and conducting discharge planning. After eighteen months, MercyOne has seen improvements in patient safety, quality, and satisfaction; increased clinician satisfaction; and higher productivity.

Some health systems have consolidated care through virtual intensive care units. Bedside robots now enable remote care that eliminates the need for on-site specialists. Videos can be used to provide preoperative education and discharge instructions, thus increasing compliance because they are available on demand for review by patients.

Conroy says many innovative health systems are devoting considerable resources to delivering a digital experience, which could also reduce the need for certain workers. "Years ago, no one thought it was possible to book airline flights directly," she notes. "Now, that's the norm. I believe that scheduling medical appointments could be done the same way." Washington-based

Providence has proven this concept with a solution called DexCare, which matches patients seeking a a clinician with a Providence provider who has open appointments. After five years of incubation, Providence spun DexCare out into the digital health market to help health systems match capacity with digital demand across all lines of care. DexCare minimizes the need for call-center or front-office staff to help coordinate appointments.

Conroy urges health care executives to balance these strategies in ways that meet the needs of their current workforce. She recommends that executives consider how to engage employees to be part of their workforce rather than forcing them to fit into an inflexible model of work. "For years, we offered 12-hour shifts for nurses, and many of them did not want anything different. But times have changed, and there are nurses who may not want to work 12 hours. If we can't get someone for 12 hours but can for six, we need to figure out how to make that happen. We should think with a gig-economy mentality so that once these employees come to work for our organization, we retain them." She cites how one health system uses the mobile payment service Venmo to compensate employees who volunteer for extra hours immediately after their shift, providing instant gratification.

Other organizations have set up their own in-house agency and become private contractors to nurses. Pittsburgh-based Allegheny Health Network's (AHN's) mobile internal staffing model offers nurses and technicians the option of rotating among AHN hospitals throughout the state. Yale New Haven Hospital (YNHH) developed an alternative staffing model that uses a variety of licensed and unlicensed nursing team members to support critical-care registered nurses. YNHH leaders also created flex shifts, including four-hour support role shifts, for nurses whose schedules could not accommodate a traditional-length shift.

Key Takeaways

What high-level considerations should health care executives keep in mind when redesigning work while meeting the demands of the workforce?

- Make wholescale workforce changes with your staff, not to your staff. "Your employees see the same problems you do," Conroy notes. "You may find that people are ready for a new way of work, and they'll embrace it."
- Remote work is making heath care executives reevaluate historical concepts of employment. "There are both positive and negative aspects to these trends," Conroy acknowledges. "But overall, offering remote work will make us better employers."

- Find ways to accommodate the gig-economy mentality of today's workers. "We're just beginning to understand what that means for us as employers," Conroy says. "What benefits matter most to employees at different stages of their lives? Is it mobility to travel, childcare, flexible shifts, or student loan forgiveness? We're at a point where we need to reevaluate what benefits people actually want and need so we can retain them as long as possible."

Conclusion

Conroy concludes, "We are seeing the emergence of a very different workforce than what we have been used to. Many of us had employees who spent their entire careers with us, and that's probably not going to be true in the future." Conroy recommends that executives adapt to the changing times. "It will be our responsibility to find ways to ensure we have the people, processes, and technologies in place to provide quality patient care, whatever that looks like, in the future."

References

HealthData.gov. 2020. "COVID-19 Reported Patient Impact and Hospital Capacity by State Timeseries (RAW)." Updated August 28, 2023. http://healthdata.gov/Hospital/COVID-19-Reported-Patient-Impact-and-Hospital-Capa/g62h-syeh.

National Council of State Boards of Nursing. 2023. "NCSBN Research Projects Significant Nursing Workforce Shortages and Crisis." Published April 13. http://ncsbn.org/news/ncsbn-research-projects-significant-nursing-workforce-shortages-and-crisis.

From the Waiting Room to the Living Room

with Scott Rissmiller, MD, Atrium Health

The practice of making house calls may seem like a quaint and nostalgic concept, but it is quickly becoming one of the most disruptive solutions for advancing health care in the United States. Although the hospital-at-home model existed before 2020, the COVID pandemic highlighted how safe and efficacious even hospital-level medical care can be when delivered in the home setting.

"Necessity is the mother of invention, or in this case, innovation," states Scott Rissmiller, MD, executive vice president and chief physician executive for Advocate Health, which is the fifth-largest integrated nonprofit health system in the nation and is headquartered in Charlotte, North Carolina. Rissmiller is widely regarded as a leader in the field of telemedicine through his work leading Charlotte-based Atrium Health, which is a part of Advocate Health.

"Atrium Health had been investing in building up our existing home health services, mobile integrated health, and other various aspects of home-based and virtual care for more than a decade prior to the pandemic," Rissmiller says.

"During COVID, rather than admitting patients, we found a vendor who helped us figure out a way to safely and successfully observe COVID patients' status in their homes, conserving much-needed hospital bedspace and personal protective equipment.

"Our clinicians then built clinical pathways for the management of these patients," he adds. "Included in this, we developed a way to provide acute care in the home using telemedicine to communicate back and forth with physicians and nurses who were tracking their patients' condition, supplemented by twice-daily visits from paramedics. We observed and treated tens of thousands of patients in this way and brought more beds online by including our own patients' actual beds."

This initiative has proven so successful that additional investments have

About the Subject Matter Expert

Scott Rissmiller, MD, is the executive vice president and chief physician executive for Advocate Health, which is the fifth-largest nonprofit, integrated health system in the United States and was created from the combination of Advocate Aurora Health and Atrium Health in December 2022. Advocate Health is a national leader in clinical innovation, health outcomes, consumer experience, and value-based care, with Wake Forest University School of Medicine serving as the academic core of the enterprise.

Under Dr. Rissmiller's leadership, Atrium Health has consistently been a top performer in providing quality care to patients when compared nationally. Dr. Rissmiller is widely regarded as a leader in the field of telemedicine, and he was included in the 2021 and 2022 classes of Modern Healthcare's "50 Most Influential Clinical Executives." Additionally, Dr. Rissmiller's expertise and insights are in frequent demand by local and national media, including Fox News, Bloomberg TV, and *The Wall Street Journal*. He was previously named as a Top 10 Hospitalist nationally by the American College of Physicians, to *Business North Carolina Magazine*'s Best Doctors list, and as *Charlotte Magazine*'s Top Doctor.

been made into remote patient monitoring, employing easy-to-use wearable devices to provide an ongoing stream of information related to the patients' vital signs and truly make possible hospital-level care in the comfort of the patient's home. Atrium Health now treats a wide variety of conditions with its hospital-at-home program, including heart failure, chronic obstructive pulmonary disease, pneumonia, asthma, and various infections and post-operative conditions.

"Our information technology experts have also created the connectivity to document vital signs and corresponding treatments in our patients' electronic medical records," Rissmiller adds.

The Changing Health Care Environment

Today's consumers expect more of their services to be personalized, on-demand, and delivered to their homes. "Our experience has been that once patients try hospital-at-home services, they prefer to never go back to on-site care,"

says Rissmiller. "Our hospital-at-home patient-experience scores are higher than our inpatient scores."

Both the financial and the clinical outcomes of Atrium Health's hospital-at-home services reflect significant efficiencies and improved quality of care:

- In 2022, readmission rates for hospital-at-home patients were 9 percent, compared with 12 percent for inpatients.
- In terms of an overall rating, patient-experience scores and "likely to recommend" scores both were double-digit percentages higher for hospital-at-home patients versus inpatient scores.
- Cost savings for hospital-at-home care equated to 25 percent of the cost of caring for inpatients.
- The hospital-at-home program saved over 25,000 bed days overs the past three years.

Atrium Health's hospital-at-home program is currently designed to serve

up to 100 patients at a time—the equivalent of eliminating much of the overhead cost of operating a midsized hospital.

Health care executives are also finding that hospital-at-home services advance some of the most critical access goals in the country. Delivering care in the home can greatly improve health equity by providing the opportunity to observe firsthand how social determinants of health (SDOH) are affecting patients.

"Many people are reluctant to share, in an office setting, how they may be having to choose between food or medications," Rissmiller notes. "By seeing the needs firsthand, we can proactively link patients with the resources they need to stay healthy."

The Centers for Medicare & Medicaid Services (CMS) waiver, which was initiated during the pandemic and provides a full inpatient diagnosis-related group payment for hospital-at-home services, is also improving care in rural settings. To receive specialized care,

Case Study: UMass Memorial Health

Capacity issues were the primary impetus for UMass Memorial Health in Worcester, Massachusetts, to develop its hospital-at-home program in March 2021 (UMass Memorial Health 2022). The health system provides care to more than half of the Medicaid population in the region and was consistently operating at or near capacity. Leaders set a goal of creating 50 new beds within the hospital-at-home care model while improving health equity among its dual-eligible patients, many with multiple comorbidities or language and access barriers. Additional challenges included a lack of broadband internet access in one-third of low-income households within the community, a low level of technical literacy, and a need to deliver services in a language other than English for 23 percent of its patients.

Within six months, the hospital-at-home team had identified and onboarded a single vendor who set up a clinical command center for the continuous monitoring of patients through technology embedded in their home. The program utilized a team of field nurses and

paramedics to complete daily home visits for each patient. In addition, patients were provided access to on-demand video calls with their care team and a translator, if necessary. An in-depth integration with UMass's electronic medical record documents real-time updates on patients' conditions. Home health hubs allow for the inclusion of patients without high-speed internet at home, supporting UMass's goals concerning patient equity.

In the first year, the UMass hospital-at-home program grew to a daily census of 12 to 16 patients. The data showed marked improvements in several metrics for hospital-at-home patients. Readmission rates were 20 to 30 percent lower than for hospital inpatients. For dual-eligible individuals, the readmission rate was less than 8 percent. Patients reported higher satisfaction in their communication with doctors and nurses and their care transitions, and were more likely overall to recommend the experience. From a capacity management perspective, the program saved more than 3,000 bed days from the 500 patients served by the program.

patients in remote locations often would have to be transferred out to tertiary care centers. Now specialists can connect virtually with patients in community-based hospitals to provide high-level care. This allows those hospitals to retain their patients and receive the accompanying revenue. "This was a challenge in the past because the reimbursement was not there, but the waiver changed that," Rissmiller notes.

Considerations for Health Care Leaders

Approximately 200 organizations across the nation have been granted CMS's Acute Hospital Care at Home Waiver. This funding has helped hospitals and health systems venture into hospital-at-home services in a big way. The CMS waiver that preserves current levels of reimbursement was extended through the end of 2024 as part of the end-of-year omnibus package passed in December 2022.

Despite this reprieve, hospital CEOs are unsure whether the reimbursement will remain this robust into the future. Responding to the 2023 *Futurescan* survey, the majority of CEOs (56 percent) said it was unlikely or highly unlikely that all major health care reimbursement agencies will reimburse for acute care in the home at rates comparable to equivalent in-hospital care by 2029. However, the same percentage of respondents believed that hospital-at-home services will be a growing trend, agreeing that at least 25 percent of acute care patients who would be treated as inpatients today will receive all of their equivalent care in their homes by 2029.

Health care leaders deliberating over the addition of hospital-at-home services may want to weigh the following considerations:

- **Financial investment.** While the start-up investment can be significant for hospital-at-home services, cost efficiencies can be realized over time, especially by scaling the approach over geographies, service lines, and populations. The model enables providers to monitor more patients at a time while supervising less expensive

care team members in the field. In addition, hospital-at-home services do not require the same brick-and-mortar infrastructure as inpatient services.
- **Access.** Rissmiller believes there are many long-term strategic advantages to developing hospital-at-home services. "Because we can see many more patients virtually than in person, hospital at home can be a partial solution for the nursing shortage," he states. Patients in rural areas can now receive services in their homes virtually, and the provision of mental health services remotely can help ease the shortage of behavioral health providers.

Capacity studies consistently demonstrate that there will be a shortage of hospital beds to accommodate the growing population of aging adults in this country. Statistics show the need to nearly double the number of inpatient beds by 2060 to care for the baby boomer population (Beckmann 2023). Hospital at home minimizes the need to add additional inpatient beds.

According to Rissmiller, one of the most promising access applications will be offering primary care in the virtual setting, aimed at keeping patients out of the hospital. "At the beginning of the pandemic, we converted all on-site appointments—which consistently had a no-show

rate of 25 percent—to virtual visits," Rissmiller recounts. "Almost immediately, our no-show rate dropped to 8 percent. When we looked into the reasons why, many patients noted barriers to access, such as having to take three buses to get to their clinic appointment."
- **Health equity.** Achieving health equity within disadvantaged populations requires an assessment of the prevailing SDOH that may be lacking and impacting wellness. Entering a patient's home provides the opportunity to see firsthand the issues that are preventing optimal health and to connect the individual with the right resources to address them. Atrium Health has found that hospital-at-home services have greatly improved health equity and increased the opportunity to refer patients to resources that close those gaps.
- **Safety.** For the model to be implemented successfully, ensuring patient and provider safety is paramount. Hospital-at-home services are subject to the same safety and quality requirements as inpatient care. Protocols need to be in place to ensure that team members are entering a safe environment. Creating a hospital-at-home culture of safety should include patient and provider agreements for designing a temporary living-room clinic environment

FUTURESCAN SURVEY RESULTS
Care in the Home

Health care executives from across the nation were asked how likely it is that the following will happen in their hospital or health system by 2029.

By 2029, at least 25 percent of acute care patients who today would be treated in our hospital or health system as inpatients will receive all of their equivalent acute care services in their homes.

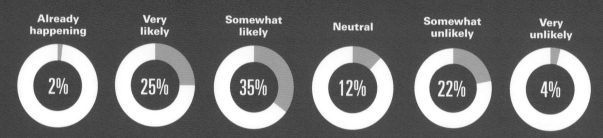

Already happening	Very likely	Somewhat likely	Neutral	Somewhat unlikely	Very unlikely
2%	25%	35%	12%	22%	4%

By 2029, all major health care reimbursement agencies, including commercial and government payers, will reimburse for acute care in the home at rates comparable to equivalent care provided in the hospital.

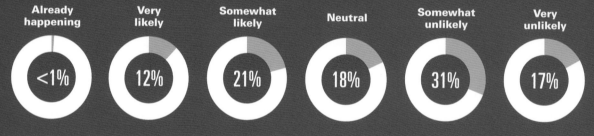

Already happening	Very likely	Somewhat likely	Neutral	Somewhat unlikely	Very unlikely
<1%	12%	21%	18%	31%	17%

and incident reporting to improve quality and processes. There should also be provider training in implicit bias, situational awareness, and de-escalation techniques.

- **Community infrastructure.** Success in this venture depends on the availability of reliable broadband connectivity to ensure in-home access to technology. Partnerships with state and local legislators may be necessary to foster community investment into infrastructure.

Key Takeaways

What are the top three questions that executives should keep in mind when evaluating or planning hospital-at-home services?

1. **Does it meet the mission of your organization?** "What patient population are you serving, and what are the goals of your health system?" Rissmiller asks. "Are you trying to solve health equity issues or capacity constraints? Like any

strategic priority, these services need to be in alignment with your vision and values."

2. **Is there buy-in?** Successful development of hospital-at-home services requires complete buy-in at all levels of the organization, from the board and C-suite to departmental leaders who will be integral to program design and execution. This includes administrators and clinicians from inpatient units and the emergency

department teams. "Most of our referrals come from these two clinical areas," Rissmiller notes. "Without their buy-in, there is a high risk of fragmentation."

3. **Are key components in place or can you develop them?** Hospital-at-home services require evidence-based care pathways, a technological infrastructure that supports remote monitoring with connectivity to the electronic health record, and quality standards that minimize variation. Multidisciplinary teams are also essential, from clinicians who can monitor patients to field care team members who provide real-time adjustments in patient care, such as administering intravenous antibiotics and other needs. Information technology infrastructure needs to be secure and seamless.

Conclusion

Hospital-at-home services are an innovative way to expand access, address health inequities, control costs, and improve the patient experience.

"Virtual health is no longer a 'nice-to-have' or an augmentation of care," states Rissmiller. "It is an essential and necessary way of delivering affordable, accessible care. COVID was the juggernaut that pushed us all out of our comfort zone. The silver lining has been the advancement of telehealth and hospital-at-home care. Coming out of it now, it has become a patient expectation to receive care this way. There's no going back to what it was before."

References

Beckmann, S. 2023. "How Inpatient Utilization Will Change Based on Population Trends." Advisory Board. Updated March 17. http://advisory.com/blog/2022/05/population-aging.

UMass Memorial Health. 2022. "UMass Memorial Health Builds Leading Hospital at Home Program." Published December 5. http://currenthealth.com/umass-memorial-health-case-study.

Sustainability Strategies

with Rod Hochman, MD, President and CEO, Providence

Climate change is having a major effect on the livability of communities throughout the United States and the world. Global warming is triggering famines, extreme heat, torrential rain, and floods and is contributing to adverse events such as hurricanes, wildfires, and tornadoes. The effects have been devastating, and scientists are warning that the worst is yet to come if countries do not make significant reductions in their greenhouse gas emissions.

The Current Health Care Landscape

Addressing the causes of climate change is a high priority for the Biden administration. In the United States, health care accounts for 8.5 percent of all emissions (The White House 2022). However, that figure includes every sector of health care, including pharmaceuticals and medical device manufacturing. According to Rod Hochman, MD, president and CEO of Providence, hospitals and health systems contribute only half of all health care emissions. Hochman is regarded as a leader in ushering health care toward more sustainable strategies. Providence employs 120,000 caregivers in 51 hospitals, 900 clinics, and a range of health and social services across Alaska, California, Montana, New Mexico, Oregon, Texas, and Washington.

Multiple factors contribute to health care organizations' carbon footprint. "Hospitals are energy-intensive enterprises," Hochman notes. "What other industry works 24/7, 365 days a year, with no downtime? Our lights are always on. The energy outlay of a hospital is about two and a half times that of a typical office building on a square-foot basis. During COVID, the care we delivered was even more supply-intensive, consuming high levels of bandages, syringes, and personal protective equipment." Hochman adds that much of the waste that hospitals produce cannot be sent to the local landfill—it requires specialized disposal methods. Yet even with the increased use of medical supplies, hospital and health system costs are still driven primarily by personnel, who account for 53 percent of all expenses. This affects financial outlay and produces waste when providing meals to both patients and employees. In 2022 alone, Providence produced 5 million meals.

About the Subject Matter Expert

Rod Hochman, MD, is the president and CEO of Providence. In this role, he is responsible for leading the seven-state health system, ensuring that access to high-quality, compassionate, and affordable care is available in each of the communities Providence serves.

Dr. Hochman is the immediate past board chair of the American Hospital Association, and he also served as board chair for the Catholic Health Association of the United States. Prior to serving as CEO of Providence, Dr. Hochman led Swedish Health Services, a Seattle-based health system that is now part of the Providence family of organizations.

Dr. Hochman received his bachelor's and medical degrees from Boston University and served as a clinical Fellow in internal medicine at Harvard Medical School and Dartmouth Medical School. He is also a Fellow of the American College of Physicians and of the American College of Rheumatology.

To mitigate these effects, Providence has committed to being carbon negative by 2030 and was one of the first health systems to sign the White House/HHS Health Sector Climate Pledge. A voluntary initiative aimed at climate resilience and emissions reduction, the pledge commits signatories to cut 50 percent of their greenhouse gas generation by 2030 and achieve net zero emissions by 2050. A group of 116 organizations representing 872 hospitals have signed the pledge as of April 12, 2023.

Key Considerations for Health Care Leaders

In order to attain the goals for reducing its carbon footprint, Providence formulated the WE ACT framework in 2020 and has been developing its scorecard in an effort to address and measure its impact in five categories:

1. Waste
2. Energy and water
3. Agriculture and food
4. Chemicals
5. Transportation

The scorecard summarizes the data that Providence collects systemwide. A variety of projects are in place that address each component of the WE ACT framework. "In 2022, Providence created 94 million pounds of waste from 52 hospitals and clinics," Hochman says. "We also use a lot of noxious chemicals, including gases for anesthesia. These are all areas where we feel we can make a meaningful impact on the path to becoming carbon negative."

Providence was an early adopter in understanding its environmental impact. It referred to the international Greenhouse Gas Protocol (GHG)—15 standards that are used for carbon accounting around the world and are not unique to health care—early on when assessing its output of emissions. The GHG protocol denotes Scope 1 emissions as direct emissions from fuels combusted by owned or leased equipment. Scope 2 emissions are indirect emissions from the generation of purchased electricity and steam. Scope 3 emissions are indirect emissions (not

included in Scope 2) that occur in the value chain of the reporting company, including both upstream and downstream emissions. The use of anesthetic gases with lower emissions is a Scope 1 goal that will have a significant effect on the output of emissions. Desflurane, a highly fluorinated ethyl methyl ether used for maintenance of general anesthesia, is a potent greenhouse gas, as is nitrous oxide. Clinicians at Providence are using anesthetic gases with lower emissions. Waste in the operating room was also a concern.

"We did a study on the contents of surgical trays before and after operations were performed," Hochman states. "We found that the number of components that were actually used was minimal compared to those that were either thrown away or reprocessed. Now we're streamlining the contents of trays depending on the needs of the surgeon."

Other ongoing efforts relate to Providence hospitals' overall infrastructure. "A number of projects are helping to reduce our energy consumption," Hochman notes. "Systemwide, we are looking at the energy efficiency of our hospitals compared to best practices, using tools like Energy Star. This identifies the opportunity for deep energy retrofits, like the installation of LED lighting and automated building systems, and updating or replacing heavy equipment like boilers to maximize efficiency. We

have also started purchasing electricity from renewable sources."

Using fewer resources per square foot and per employee is an overarching goal. Providence virtualized as many positions as it could when the pandemic began and minimized travel for meetings. These measures eliminated work commutes and air travel, policies that continue now that the pandemic is over.

"We are also in the process of converting our fleets of vehicles to electric vehicles," Hochman says. "We are saving a lot of money on cars, fuel, and airfare, and minimizing their use also saves the environment. Changing out equipment and lights to be more energy-efficient is lowering expenses on electricity. The bottom line is, we need to look comprehensively at all the options for reducing our carbon emissions. We are also challenging our pharmaceutical and medical device suppliers to consider what they are doing to minimize their own carbon footprint." Hochman says that through its various green initiatives, Providence saved $11 million in 2022. By 2030, the goal is to save $100 million each year through improved practices and purchases.

As a faith-based system guided by values, Providence has a moral imperative to minimize its contribution to climate change as much as possible. "The pope issued an encyclical on the environment, and as a Catholic system, we need to pay attention to it," states

Hochman. He also cites a September 2021 consensus statement from more than 200 medical journals that named climate change as the number-one threat to global public health. "Patients are being impacted by climate change. And unfortunately, it disproportionally affects people at the lower end of the socioeconomic spectrum," he notes. "Health equity is tied to climate change, which is directly related to health. We have a societal and moral obligation to try to minimize the diseases and conditions that stem from global warming."

Cooperation and coordination among health systems around the country are at an all-time high in the mitigation of climate change. In addition to the numerous organizations that have taken the Health Sector Climate Pledge advanced by the Biden administration, Hochman sees hospitals learning from each other. "Health care organizations in the same region are coordinating on energy consumption and on buying energy together. They're adopting new methods of waste management. Collectively, we have a great ability to impact suppliers. A big incentive to work together is addressing health care's carbon footprint before it becomes a mandate. We can be part of the process and educate legislators on what makes us different and what we can realistically achieve on our own."

Other health systems have also been devoting considerable resources to developing sustainability strategies that help mitigate emissions and reduce waste.

Case Study: Gundersen Health System

Gundersen Health System, which includes seven hospitals and 65 clinics serving patients in Wisconsin, Minnesota, and Iowa, founded the Gundersen Envision program in 2008. The program is aimed at improving the health of the communities it serves and controlling rising energy costs by reducing consumption through improved efficiency and the creation of cleaner energy. Gundersen Envision has invested nearly $30 million in renewable-energy

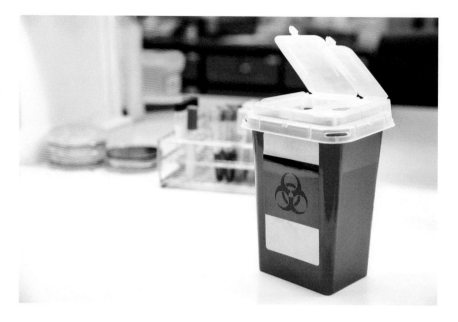

projects that have focused on biogas, geothermal, landfill gas, solar, wind, and more. Over the last 10 years, Gundersen's energy conservation efforts have resulted in a cumulative financial savings of more than $28 million—a 54 percent improvement—and annual savings of nearly $2 million. The system's 67 percent recycling and diversion rate has been attained through the following measures:

- Donating over 6,000 meals that otherwise would have become part of the waste stream.
- Recycling 477 tons of paper and cardboard, enough to replenish more than 6,000 trees in just one year.
- Donating more than 74,000 pounds of medical supplies, equipment, and furniture to more than 20 charitable organizations.

In 2014, Gundersen became the first energy-independent hospital in the country.

Case Study: The Ohio State University Wexner Medical Center

The Ohio State University Wexner Medical Center (OSUWMC) has successfully diverted 50 tons of plastic each year by repurposing reusable containers for items with sharp points, such as needles, syringes, and finger-stick devices

to draw blood. As with many hospitals, OSUWMC uses thousands of sharps containers in exam rooms, operating rooms, and other locations, and its routine practice had been to trash each container when it was full for safety and sanitary reasons.

The OSUWMC sustainability team felt that many of the containers could be reused. A pilot was introduced where the contents of new containers were safely disposed of through a vendor, who then cleaned the containers and put them back into circulation. Each container can be used up to 600 times. The test was so successful that the policy was expanded throughout the medical center. OSUWMC reports that this process kept more than 150,000 sharps containers out of landfills in 2021 (Boyle 2022).

Clearly, even small initiatives can have a significant effect. The issue of minimizing greenhouse gases is starting to take hold in C-suites across the country. According to the results of the latest *Futurescan* survey, 43 percent of health care leaders said it was very or somewhat likely that their organizations will have reduced their Scope 1 and Scope 2 emissions by at least 15 percent by 2029 through the implementation of sustainability solutions. Nearly the same percentage—42 percent—believed that it was somewhat or very likely that their hospitals or health systems would have

FUTURESCAN SURVEY RESULTS
Sustainability

Health care executives from across the nation were asked how likely it is that the following will happen in their hospital or health system by 2029.

By 2029, our hospital or health system will have reduced its Scope 1 and Scope 2 emissions by at least 15 percent as a result of implementing sustainability solutions.

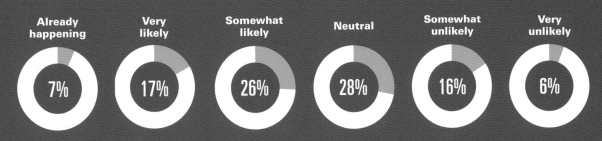

Already happening	Very likely	Somewhat likely	Neutral	Somewhat unlikely	Very unlikely
7%	17%	26%	28%	16%	6%

By 2029, our hospital or health system will have a comprehensive plan in place to reduce Scope 3 emissions.

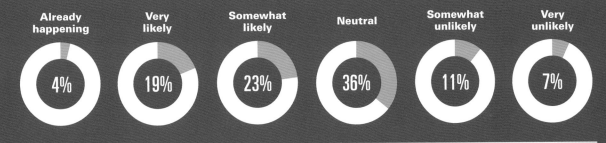

Already happening	Very likely	Somewhat likely	Neutral	Somewhat unlikely	Very unlikely
4%	19%	23%	36%	11%	7%

a comprehensive plan in place to reduce Scope 3 emissions by 2029.

Key Takeaways

Hochman delineates several principles for success for health care executives who want to initiate efforts to lower their organizations' carbon footprint.

- **Take personal responsibility for the initiative.** "Everyone, from the board of directors to the leadership team down to rank-and-file employees, needs to see this as a priority," Hochman advises. "People need to commit to addressing this on an everyday basis."

- **Identify a champion.** It is essential that someone in the organization is accountable for the overarching mission and answers directly to the CEO. "It could be the chief operating officer or chief financial officer, but it needs to be someone who has eyes and ears on the strategy of the organization," Hochman notes. "Leadership by committee doesn't work; this effort is complex and requires someone to organize the efforts. It can't be a part-time role. You also need content experts who understand, for example, how energy consumption is measured and rated using established environmental impact methodologies."

- **Determine priorities and how to measure success.** "Look at the obvious low-hanging fruit, such as waste or energy consumption. A first effort could be as simple as changing out the light bulbs," Hochman says. "Recycling is very popular among our caregivers, and optimizing our waste streams can result in lower purchasing in the first place. The national average waste of food is 30 to 40 percent—another excellent metric to tackle. All these projects can have a positive effect on the bottom line and contribute to cost savings while connecting to our mission and meeting our obligation to our communities."

Once the initiatives have been identified, it is essential to measure the organization's current consumption and rate of waste. "This is the framework by which you can measure your progress," notes Hochman. Providence's WE ACT scorecard is a one-of-a-kind database that measures 40 different elements of environmental stewardship. It includes metrics such as kilowatt hours, gallons of water used, carbon emissions, the percentage of food used that is sustainably produced, and purchasing statistics. The scorecard is generated monthly from every Providence hospital and soon will be produced by the system's non-acute sites as well. Already, its acute care facilities are capturing data for 80 percent of their intended metrics. "The WE ACT scorecard is evidence based and data driven. Everyone can see and understand so much more about consumption in a very complex organization," states Hochman. "I think this is going to be a gold standard. Remember: You can't fix what you don't measure."

- **Consider green design in facility planning.** "The facilities we build are constructed with energy efficiency in mind," notes Hochman. "That includes everything from the use of sustainable materials during construction to the placement of operating rooms and supplies. We also look at each location to determine its resilience during a catastrophic event such as earthquakes and flooding."

Conclusion

Hochman emphasizes that hospitals and health systems have many reasons to prioritize green initiatives: "We have a moral and social obligation to understand how climate change is affecting the communities we serve. Health care organizations need to lead the discussions and work that address how climate change impacts the health of people. Reducing our carbon footprint shouldn't be a chore. The goals are so much a part of what we do, and the future of our children and grandchildren depends on it."

References

Boyle, P. 2022. "Hospitals Take Creative Steps to Reduce Carbon Footprint." Association of American Medical Colleges. Published July 28. http://aamc.org/news/hospitals-take-creative-steps-reduce-carbon-footprint.

The White House. 2022. "Fact Sheet: Health Sector Leaders Join Biden Administration's Pledge to Reduce Greenhouse Gas Emissions 50% by 2030." Briefing Room. Published June 30. http://whitehouse.gov/briefing-room/statements-releases/2022/06/30/fact-sheet-health-sector-leaders-join-biden-administrations-pledge-to-reduce-greenhouse-gas-emissions-50-by-2030.

The Future of Population and Public Health

with Omar Lateef, DO, President and CEO of RUSH; and David A. Ansell, MD, MPH, RUSH Senior Vice President for Community Health Equity

Does the term *population health* refer to the health of patients seen by hospitals and health systems or to the health of people within the entire region of a service area? These two groups are not analogous, according to Omar Lateef, DO, president and chief executive officer (CEO) of RUSH, an academic health system in the Chicago area that includes RUSH University Medical Center, RUSH Copley Medical Center, RUSH Oak Park Hospital, RUSH University, and an extensive network of providers and outpatient care facilities. "Sometimes, they're not even close to being the same population," Lateef adds.

In reality, population health encompasses not only the patients who entrust their care to a hospital or health system but also the well-being of the community from which those patients come. Understanding such distinctions is vital for ensuring that medical needs are addressed equitably at both an individual and a community level.

The Current Health Care Landscape

According to David Ansell, MD, MPH, the provision of health care in the United States has been driven primarily by the fragmented public and private payor systems intended to fund it, but the variables in coverage and payment have contributed to unsatisfactory outcomes, particularly in communities of color. Ansell serves as senior vice president for community health equity for RUSH University Medical Center.

"The payment rates set by Medicare and especially Medicaid are often inadequate to fully reimburse hospitals and providers for the services they provide," Ansell says. "Many physicians don't even take Medicaid. Yet many low-income patients rely on Medicaid, and they are usually the same populations who struggle with adverse social determinants of health, which make accessing health care services a challenge." Of course, some states still have not expanded Medicaid coverage, and their uninsured populations—often disproportionately people of color—have great difficulty accessing care. The payment system is just one factor that has contributed to poorer outcomes.

Both Lateef and Ansell maintain that racial health inequity is a public

About the Subject Matter Experts

Omar Lateef, DO, has led the RUSH team into the future of health care with a steadfast eye on quality and equity. He has served as president and chief executive officer of RUSH University Medical Center since May 2019, was appointed president of RUSH in 2021, and became RUSH's CEO in July 2022. Prior to becoming president and CEO of RUSH University Medical Center, Lateef was its chief medical officer.

Under his leadership, RUSH has set the nation's standard in health care quality and safety, modeled excellence in clinical leadership both regionally and nationally, and maintained its deep and long-standing commitment to health equity. RUSH leaders, along with others across the nation, educate the world's top health care professionals. RUSH is laser-focused on serving its patients and communities by addressing the root causes of disease through strong partnerships and innovative research.

David Ansell, MD, MPH, is the Michael E. Kelly Presidential Professor of Internal Medicine and senior vice president/associate provost for community health equity at RUSH University Medical Center in Chicago. He is a 1978 graduate of SUNY Upstate Medical College and did his medical training at Cook County Hospital in Chicago. He spent 13 years at Cook County as an attending physician and ultimately was appointed chief of the division of general internal medicine there. From 1995 to 2005 he was chairman of internal medicine at Chicago's Mount Sinai Hospital. He was recruited to Rush University Medical Center as its inaugural chief medical officer in 2005, a position he held until 2015. His research and advocacy have been focused on eliminating health inequities. In 2011 he published a memoir of his times at Cook County Hospital titled *County: Life, Death and Politics at Chicago's Public Hospital.* His latest book, *The Death Gap: How Inequality Kills*, was published in 2017.

health crisis in the United States. "It is undeniable that racism is a root cause of health inequity," Lateef says. "But it is not enough to simply say it. There needs to be more integration between care provision and addressing the social determinants of health, which collectively impact 50 to 60 percent of a person's well-being."

In a pivotal move designed to address this, both the Centers for Medicare & Medicaid Services and The Joint Commission are now requiring health systems to ascertain social needs among their patients, including food insecurity and homelessness.

Addressing Racial Inequity

Lateef and Ansell believe that merging strategies that are focused on patient populations with community-based and public health initiatives will be key for addressing the health inequities that affect historically marginalized communities. Impacting health inequities will also require intentional investment from health systems, which are often the largest businesses and employers in their communities, to stimulate economic growth via anchor strategies.

Initially conceptualized by the Aspen Institute in 2001, an anchor strategy is a place-based business approach to building community health and wealth by means of local hiring, investing, purchasing, and community engagement. The anchor strategy movement has gained increasing momentum in health care. For RUSH, the impetus to adopt an anchor strategy was its 2016 community health needs assessment, which identified structural racism and economic deprivation as among the root causes of a 16-year life-expectancy gap between Chicago's largely White lakeshore community and the largely Black population of Garfield Park on its West Side (Ansell, Fruin, et al. 2023). As the largest employer in the area, RUSH's leadership team believed it had a responsibility to address the structural factors affecting health within Chicago's West Side communities (see exhibit 1).

Launched in 2017, RUSH's anchor strategy focused first and foremost on impacting the lives of its employees who

live in West Side neighborhoods. It set annual targets for increasing local

- hiring,
- career pathways,
- purchasing and business development efforts,
- investments in community-building efforts, and
- volunteering.

Numerous initiatives to build community health and wealth fell under these five pillars. Data collected internally showed that RUSH's employees in these neighborhoods had the highest rates of financial distress, including emergency withdrawals from retirement accounts and low participation in those plans.

By 2021, contributions rose to nearly 80 percent, up from 34 percent in 2017. Other positive effects included the following:

- Hiring of individuals from target communities increased from 16 percent of all hires in 2018 to 18 percent in 2021.
- By 2021, 88 percent of RUSH employees were earning more than the regional living wage.
- A major supplier of medical equipment to the health care industry agreed to construct a 65,000-square-foot distribution center in a West Side neighborhood in exchange

for a purchasing contract with RUSH, boosting local employment significantly.

In 2018, RUSH was joined by five other health systems to establish West Side United (WSU), a racial-equity collaborative formed to benefit Chicago's 500,000 West Side residents.

Since 2018, collectively the WSU members have

- invested $10.8 million through community-development financial institutions to fund businesses, nonprofits, and affordable housing;
- raised $3 million to establish four health care career pathways;
- raised $1.9 million to support local businesses; and
- provided business-development support to 150 West Side businesses and 60 community-based organizations (Ansell, Oliver-Hightower, et al. 2021).

The Intersection of Population Health and Public Health

The extent of racial health disparities was never more evident than during the COVID-19 pandemic. "Blacks, Latinos, and Native American were three times more likely to contract COVID and twice as likely to die from it than Whites," Ansell says." The pandemic also demonstrated the critical need for closer alignment between public health and the care delivery system."

Ansell notes that COVID required a response far beyond inpatient care. "The community needed an infrastructure to distribute masks and testing kits, and to administer vaccinations," he says. "As a health system, we looked to clinics, community health centers, and community-based organizations to assist in this process because the public health infrastructure wasn't there."

These lessons learned during the pandemic highlight the need to create closer hospital partnerships with public health departments and community organizations. "We need a federated system of population health to be able to respond in an integrated way to the next public health emergency," Lateef states. "Building one shared database for disease and outbreak surveillance is an area that needs to be developed. Hospitals already have epidemiologists and track this information internally. A public–private system to build and

maintain labs and an information technology infrastructure is also critical." According to the latest *Futurescan* survey, the majority of hospital and health system leaders (57 percent) also see this need and say their organizations already have—or soon will have—shared-data agreements with community organizations to better analyze and predict

the health status and needs of local residents.

"There should also be collaboration around community health priorities such as maternal health or chronic conditions to help focus on those populations that have been historically marginalized," says Lateef. He suggests that in the future, there should be

Exhibit 1

The Evolution of RUSH's Anchor Strategy

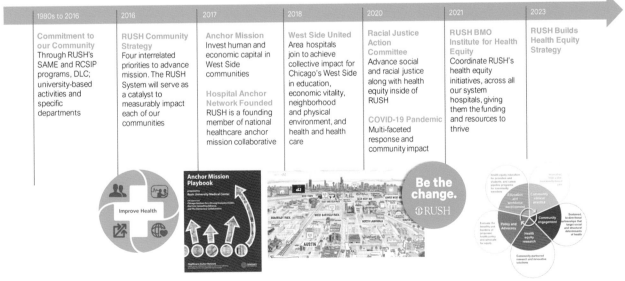

1980s to 2016	2016	2017	2018	2020	2021	2023
Commitment to our Community Through RUSH's SAME and RCSIP programs, DLC; university-based activities and specific departments	**RUSH Community Strategy** Four interrelated priorities to advance mission. The RUSH System will serve as a catalyst to measurably impact each of our communities	**Anchor Mission** Invest human and economic capital in West Side communities	**West Side United** Area hospitals join to achieve collective impact for Chicago's West Side in education, economic vitality, neighborhood and physical environment, and health and health care	**Racial Justice Action Committee** Advance social and racial justice along with health equity inside of RUSH	**RUSH BMO Institute for Health Equity** Coordinate RUSH's health equity initiatives, across all our system hospitals, giving them the funding and resources to thrive	**RUSH Builds Health Equity Strategy**
		Hospital Anchor Network Founded RUSH is a founding member of national healthcare anchor mission collaborative		**COVID-19 Pandemic** Multi-faceted response and community impact		

⬙ RUSH

FUTURESCAN SURVEY RESULTS
Population Health

Health care executives from across the nation were asked how likely it is that the following will happen in their hospital or health system by 2029.

By 2029, our hospital or health system will have established an anchor strategy that includes effective community partnerships to address community and population health.

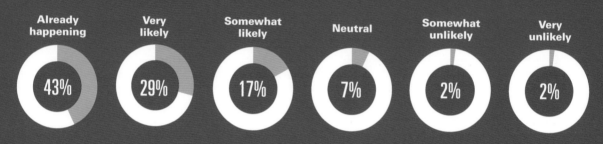

Already happening	Very likely	Somewhat likely	Neutral	Somewhat unlikely	Very unlikely
43%	29%	17%	7%	2%	2%

By 2029, our hospital or health system will have implemented shared data agreements with community organizations to better analyze and predict the health status and needs of our communities.

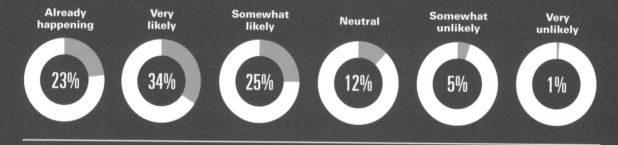

Already happening	Very likely	Somewhat likely	Neutral	Somewhat unlikely	Very unlikely
23%	34%	25%	12%	5%	1%

greater alignment in messaging about safety measures, precautions, and access to care in a public health crisis.

Direct community wealth-building investments from hospitals also are needed. RUSH and its community partners in the Garfield Park Rite to Wellness Collaborative were recently named the winners of the prestigious Chicago Prize, a $10 million philanthropic gift directed to support the building of the Sankofa Wellness

Village, a complex of health-related investments that RUSH helped spearhead in the community on Chicago's West Side with the lowest life expectancy. This $40 million capital investment project includes significant contributions from RUSH.

Forward-thinking health care executives are going beyond community health assessments to advocate for public health funding to create infrastructure projects like these for advancing joint

initiatives that promote population health. Like RUSH, Kaiser Permanente, and Intermountain Healthcare (see sidebar on page 25), health systems across the country are starting to adopt an anchor strategy within their own communities. Over 43 percent of health care leaders said in response to the 2023 *Futurescan* survey that they already have such a strategy in place; 46 percent said it was likely or very likely that they would have one in place by 2029.

Key Takeaways

RUSH's leadership team suggests the following takeaways as health care leaders plan their organizations' population and public health initiatives:

- Consider becoming an anchor health care institution. Traditionally, hospital leaders have viewed racial inequities as being out of a health system's control. An anchor strategy builds on already-existing hospital operations—hiring, purchasing, and investing—in a manner that creates place-based wealth and health for residents of the community in which the hospital does business. "This is definitely within a health system's realm of responsibility," Lateef notes.

- Screen all patients for social determinants of health. Knowing what the biggest community deficits are (e.g., transportation, fresh food, homelessness) is the first step to addressing population health issues and poor outcomes.

Case Study: Intermountain Healthcare Local Impact Investing

Established in 2017, the Healthcare Anchor Network (HAN) is a health system–led collaboration focused on improving health and well-being by building more inclusive and sustainable local economies. Member organizations pledge to invest in low-income neighborhoods and communities of color, addressing not just health disparities but also economic and racial inequities. Intermountain Healthcare is a nonprofit health system based in Salt Lake City, Utah, that serves patients and communities in Utah, Idaho, and Nevada and operates 33 hospitals. The health system began evolving its role as an anchor institution in 2019 through its community health needs assessment. That year, Intermountain signed HAN's Place-Based Investment Commitment and allocated up to 2 percent of its overall investment portfolio to local-impact projects.

One investment project of the program is the Utah Housing Preservation Fund, which aims to address Utah's housing crisis by spending $100 million to prevent subsidized and naturally occurring affordable housing from being converted to market-rate rentals. The Preservation Fund was created in March 2020 and consists of private institutions that collectively provided $20 million in total, $4 million of which was provided by Intermountain. In 2020, the Preservation Fund constructed or preserved 491 housing units, 82 of which are located in rural areas and 206 of which are for residents earning 50 percent or less of the area's median income. The Preservation Fund intends to measure the success of these investments through community health outcomes, which will be measured by a survey of residents on perceived well-being, financial security, and feelings of hope.

As of 2021, Intermountain deployed $23 million, with 80 percent of its investments directed to affordable housing. The remaining 20 percent of its investment helps support small businesses and behavioral health nonprofits. The assets allocated to impact investing target a rate of return of between 2 and 4 percent in order to preserve the real value of the impact-investing portfolio. A return of principal is expected for all investments, and the portfolio in aggregate is expected to match or exceed inflation (HAN 2021b).

Case Study: Kaiser Permanente Thriving Communities Fund

As a founding member of HAN, Kaiser Permanente committed to expend $200 million of unrestricted net assets for place-based impact investments by 2024. It exceeded that pledge and met the goal early, investing $220 million by the end of 2020. Affordable housing investments make up 80 percent of Kaiser Permanente's impact investments, with the other 20 percent committed to economic development.

One impact investment in Kaiser's portfolio is the Housing for Health Fund, which provides equity capital to help preserve affordable housing in the San Francisco Bay Area and Sacramento. The fund helps developers purchase naturally occurring affordable and aging Low-Income Housing Tax Credit (LIHTC) multi-unit housing, effectively protecting residents from rent increases and possible eviction. Another project, the Supportive Housing Fund, is directed at building up to 1,800 financially sustainable permanent supportive housing (PSH) units for people experiencing homelessness in California. The fund's approach will allow for PSH to be rapidly developed statewide, but predominantly in the Los Angeles area, which has a significant and growing homeless population (HAN 2021a).

- Create novel partnerships. "No one hospital or health system can tackle these issues alone," Ansell states. He suggests opening a dialogue with the local public health department, other health systems that are engaged in addressing community needs, and community businesses and nonprofits. "Partnering with federally qualified health centers in your region can also help make care available beyond the emergency room," he adds.
- Advocate for payment reform nationally. "We currently have a tale of two Americas: those who are middle-class with insurance and those without," Lateef says. "Medicaid needs to raise its rates because it creates inherent health inequity in populations without any other type of insurance." He also urges health care executives to revisit their own policies on accepting Medicare and Medicaid.

Conclusion

Health care executives can have the biggest impact on the future of population and public health by eliminating health inequities and the root causes that contribute to them: poverty and systemic racism. "Most CEOs want to do more than balance the books," notes Lateef. "No one goes into health care to say, 'We made a profit every year.' I believe that most of us want to be able to say, 'We saved lives.' The creation of health and wealth using a health system's resources can accomplish that and more. It creates hope for the next generation."

References

Ansell, D. A., K. Fruin, R. Holman, A. Jaco, B. H. Pham, and D. Zuckerman. 2023. "The Anchor Strategy—A Place-Based Business Approach for Health Equity." *New England Journal of Medicine*. Published January 12. http://nejm.org/doi/full/10.1056/NEJMp2213465.

Ansell, D. A., D. Oliver-Hightower, L. J. Goodman, O. B. Lateef, and T. J. Johnson. 2021. "Health Equity as a System Strategy: The Rush University Medical Center Framework." *NEJM Catalyst*. Published April 21. http://catalyst.nejm.org/doi/full/10.1056/CAT.20.0674.

Healthcare Anchor Network (HAN). 2021a. "Case Study—Kaiser Permanente: Thriving Communities Fund." Published July 28. https://healthcareanchor.network/2021/07/kaiser-permanente-thriving-communities-fund.

———. 2021b. "Case Study—Intermountain Healthcare: Local Impact Investing." Published October 6. https://healthcareanchor.network/wp-content/uploads/2021/07/Intermountain-PBI-Case-Study_3.pdf.

Direct Contracting with Employers

with Jane Thornhill, MSA, Vice President of Business Operations, Henry Ford Physician Network

Self-insured employers, frustrated with the cost and complexity of traditional health insurance contracts, are bypassing insurance companies to establish direct-to-employer contracts with local health systems.

Large companies such as Boeing, Disney, General Motors, Intel, Walmart, and Whole Foods have implemented direct-to-employer health care contracts to provide cost savings while maintaining or improving access to care for their employees (Mulvany 2020). A 2021 survey from the Business Group on Health found that 9 percent of large employers have implemented direct contracts for primary care and almost 20 percent are considering a move to direct contracting in the near future (FTI Consulting 2022). And such strategies are not necessarily only for large companies.

In the latest *Futurescan* survey, over 40 percent of all respondents reported that their hospital or health system has already created some form of self-insured, direct-to-employer relationship between employees and health care services. In addition, nearly 35 percent of respondents said that it was either somewhat or very likely that such an

arrangement would be implemented within five years.

For health systems, this trend presents an opportunity to embrace direct contracting; however, a successful relationship can be challenging to implement and comes with risks.

Jane Thornhill, MSA—the vice president of business operations for the Henry Ford Physician Network (HFPN), which is part of Henry Ford Health in Detroit—leads a team of

administrators that seeks to increase quality of care and decrease cost of services for employees of Henry Ford Health (HFH). HFPN successfully implemented direct contracting relationships for General Motors (GM ConnectedCare) in 2019, and for its own employees at HFH in 2023. Thanks to the lessons learned from these experiences, Thornhill possesses an expert's insight into the growing trend of employer-provided health care.

About the Subject Matter Expert

Jane Thornhill, MSA, has successfully worked in various leadership roles at Henry Ford Health since joining the organization as vice president of business operations for the Henry Ford Physician Network in 2019.

In this role Thornhill is responsible for Henry Ford Physician Network's operations as well as the implementation of its strategic plan. She also plays an important role in instituting the network's governance model, which is designed to strengthen its relationships with physician

organizations throughout southeast Michigan and beyond.

Instrumental in creating Henry Ford's Referring Physician Network, Thornhill draws on past experiences by building relationships with independent physicians to further strengthen ties within the network. She returned to Henry Ford Health after consulting for Evolent Health, where she implemented primary care and specialty governance models to support value-based care initiatives.

FUTURESCAN SURVEY RESULTS
Employer Contracting

Health care executives from across the nation were asked how likely it is that the following will happen in their hospital or health system by 2029.

By 2029, our hospital or health system will have contracted directly with self-insured employers in our community to be a provider of health care to their employees, in an exclusive or partially exclusive agreement.

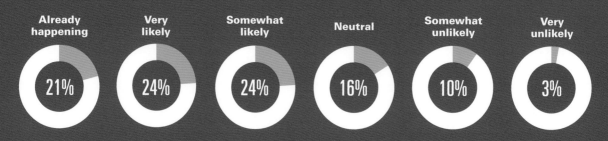

Already happening	Very likely	Somewhat likely	Neutral	Somewhat unlikely	Very unlikely
21%	24%	24%	16%	10%	3%

By 2029, our hospital or health system will have created some form of self-insured, direct-to-employer relationship between our own employees and our health care services.

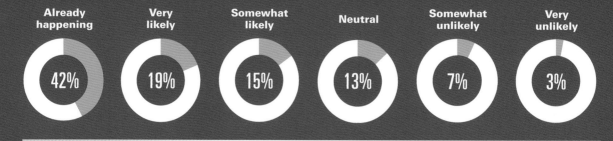

Already happening	Very likely	Somewhat likely	Neutral	Somewhat unlikely	Very unlikely
42%	19%	15%	13%	7%	3%

Benefits of Direct Contracting

Cost savings are among the many benefits of establishing a direct contracting relationship with health care providers. "Most employers are seeing year-over-year premium increases, and beneficiaries are experiencing increased out-of-pocket costs," Thornhill says. "One of the concerns is that people are pausing on care because it costs so much. You need a healthy population to perform your work function, and you want them to have quality access to care."

Direct-to-employer contracts provide the opportunity to form close relationships with the providers who are rendering care to employees and to define meaningful metrics that measure success. A direct contract gives the employer tight control over the features and outcomes that are prioritized within a health plan. In Thornhill's experience, this leads to cost savings and higher employee satisfaction, and it helps employers tangibly invest in their employees' health.

Features of a Successful Relationship

One of the benefits of a direct-to-employer contract is the ability to tailor it to a specific employee population. Identifying key features and quality metrics of success can be daunting. Thornhill provides insight into how to identify which features to include in a direct-to-employer contract and how to use quality metrics to ensure optimal outcomes (see exhibit 1).

Personalization. What should employers prioritize when developing a direct contract? Strong data analytics are necessary to gain insight into what is most appropriate for an individual company. Assess what your current plan offers and how your employees are using it, Thornhill advises.

"General Motors invested in their own internal resources to know exactly what they wanted to buy," which expedited the process, Thornhill says. Health systems that are engaged in these direct-to-employer contracts need to counsel employers to examine their health care claims data to understand the disease burden on their employees and design the services that will be needed. "Say, for instance, employers have a population of employees who are diabetic," Thornhill explains. "They are going to want to make sure that they have a contractual relationship with someone who has a very good diabetic care program."

A successful plan will not force employees to switch providers or otherwise lose access to care. Above all, Thornhill says, strive to curb out-of-pocket costs and avoid increasing deductibles. Heath care delivery systems that are entering into agreements should ask employers, *Are you seeing people delaying care, and is your employee population getting sicker?* "If that's the case, then what you really want to do is try to drive down that out-of-pocket cost and increase access to care at the right time and at the right level of care," Thornhill says. "Because in the long run, if people are delaying care, we're going in the wrong direction."

Quality metrics. Quality metrics in direct contracts hold parties accountable, and failure to meet them typically results in a financial penalty. Quality-metric goals improve care when all stakeholders are invested in the effort, Thornhill says. At HFPN, a patient's electronic medical record will note whether that person is a GM or HFH beneficiary and help providers recognize the employee's health care requirements. "If I'm going to see my dermatologist, and that dermatologist's office sees I

Exhibit 1

Designing a Successful Direct Contract

Keys to successful direct-to-employer contracting

Personalization
- What does the current health plan offer?
- How do employees use their health plans?
  - Where do employees go for care?
  - What care do employees seek?
- Does the employee population have specific needs?

Quality metrics
- Wait times
- Screening goals
- Cost targets
- Customer service goals
- Disease metrics (A1C, BMI)

haven't gotten my mammogram, it's going to flag that," Thornhill explains. "Everyone I interact with is responsible for my care."

To facilitate quality metric measurements, it is important to contract with providers who are required to share their patient data. At HFPN, providers are required to allow their patient data in the contracts to flow into HFH's electronic data warehouse. Keeping a close eye on quality metrics helps guide contractual terms. Thornhill recommends reviewing metrics monthly and holding joint operating committee meetings quarterly.

Health data also help identify waste and problem areas. With strong analysis, a company can question whether certain initiatives or plan features are truly effective. "It will show you flaws in a contract term or health care delivery workflow if you let it," Thornhill says. "Let those flaws be part of the contractual terms so it forces you to fix them." Leaders should design these terms to guide the company to attain a higher level of professional acumen.

Challenges of Direct Contract Implementation

Direct contracting can be a complex arrangement with significant challenges:

- **Specialized staff**—It takes a dedicated team of people with specialized skills—often from the human resources department—to develop a direct contract. Helping employers identify which health care services their employees need is challenging. "Watching how long it took for HFH to do this for ourselves—and we deliver health care for a living—was eye-opening," Thornhill says. Companies may also seek advice on developing a direct-to-employer contract from pharmaceutical companies or others with experience in traditional health care.

  Actuarial support to understand the risks inherent in these contracts is critical for employers. Employers must maintain a dedicated data analytics staff to perform the necessary analyses, which will elucidate how employees are using and benefiting from their health plans. "Employers want to truly understand their employee–patient population and ensure they have the analytics to support some of the decisions they are going to make," Thornhill says.

- **Understanding value**—Determining fair market value is another hurdle when establishing a direct contracting relationship, Thornhill notes. Health systems should compare the price of the features being purchased with similar companies offering similar services and should understand which elements are standard or come at extra cost.

- **Employee education**—Educational efforts help employees understand the benefits of a direct-to-employer contract, and they encourage employees to switch to it. Make it clear that the plan's features were designed with the employees' best interests in mind.

- **Mitigating risks**—Companies of all sizes can apply the principles of direct contracting to save money and improve health care access. "To be able to take on risks, the employer as well as the health system needs to have a large enough patient population to balance the risk," Thornhill says. Smaller companies that are based in the same geographic area can also collaborate on a direct contract as a group. Thornhill continues, "If you're a small employer, then get a consortium of people together. Together, you've got economies of scale."

Risk arrangements are often made using upside risk models or upside/downside risk models. In upside risk models, providers obtain a reward for improving quality and are not penalized for overspending; in upside/downside models, the overspending risk is either shared by the employer and provider or assumed by the provider. In these upside/downside models, the risk is evaluated by examining overall quality, cost, and utilization metrics to ensure the providers are incentivized for their performance above benchmarks. In Thornhill's experience, these models are effective.

Upside-only can be helpful at the beginning of a contract, Thornhill explains, and might involve the health system showing that it can perform the requested tasks for a year or two. After the employer gains insight into how the employees engage with the new health plan, introducing downside risk over

time can put more "skin in the game" for everyone concerned. Additionally, during the upside-only phase, the employees/beneficiaries should experience the benefit of decreased out-of-pocket costs, which can increase their engagement with and excitement for this type of health care plan.

"If the health system has to write the employer a check, then the health system is paying a lot more attention than when the insurance company just gets to keep whatever their savings or losses are," Thornhill notes. Setting aside a portion of saved money into a risk-mitigation pool can help offset down years, she adds.

Setting Up Your Contract: Further Considerations

Thornhill advises health system executives to consider several other aspects of a contract before setting it in motion.

- **Internal contracting**—Thornhill recommends that health systems attempt to set up a direct-to-employer contract with themselves before offering the product to others. This exercise will allow the organization to work out kinks and increase confidence and credibility. "Our employees are our most valued resource. They care for our patients— we want them to let us take care of them. Why have a plan that lets employees go somewhere else if we

believe we can give them the best care? And why wouldn't we want to do this for our most trusted and important resource?" Thornhill asks. "If you can't deliver it at home, then where's your confidence level of being able to deliver it for others?"

- **The role of the insurance company**—Insurance companies still have a role to play in direct-to-employer relationships, Thornhill notes. As third-party administrators, insurance companies have extremely valuable claims data, and employers will continue to rely on them to understand how employees use their coverage. Insurance companies are also adopting quality metrics along with cost and utilization measures to provide reimbursement incentives. "They're trying to do it themselves, but they're keeping a good chunk of the money, too," Thornhill explains.

- **Encouraging engagement**— Engagement with employer health requirements is a particular concern for health care systems, which tend to have trouble motivating their employees to seek care, Thornhill says. Concerns about privacy are important. Receiving care where you work with colleagues you know can be challenging. Personal pride and the stigma of needing care can contribute to this resistance. These barriers need to be combated. If a patient population isn't engaging with required annual care requirements (e.g., exams, screenings), the employer should charge those who are not complying more for their premium. This will encourage them to engage, Thornhill says. At first, she notes, employees at HFPN were resistant to the care requirements, but the company provided incentives and raffles to gamify the effort. "Now, it's just standard," Thornhill says. "If you don't do it by the end of March, your premiums go up."

- **Recognizing value**—Value-based care requires a holistic view of all the costs and outcomes of a patient's care and incentivizes high value over high volume. In this model, the health system and the employer share the reward of cost savings, but the benefit of this arrangement may not be apparent when viewed through a traditional fee-for-service lens. Thornhill has encountered concerns from hospital executives about decreasing emergency room admissions, which she says indicates healthier patients and is a desired outcome both in a value-based arrangement and from a patient's perspective.

   "We need to show them that those dollars are being earned elsewhere. It's a shift; it's not a complete takeaway," Thornhill says. "You have to do the internal investment for these kinds of product offerings to be able to show that the health system is keeping employees healthier. They are just doing it in a different way."

Key Takeaways

Thornhill shares three key takeaways to consider when thinking about taking advantage of a direct-to-employer contract:

- **Ask yourself: Do you want to provide direct-to-employer self-insured product offerings to your own employees?** Consider how a direct contracting relationship might look for your organization. Consider the risks and benefits of moving away from the current traditional model and how this change might affect the organization. "Just start to consider it," Thornhill says. "In those considerations come opportunities."
- **Have conversations with local health care delivery systems.** Getting to know the health care systems in the area can spark mutually beneficial partnerships, Thornhill notes. Executives should consider health care among other services they purchase, such as suppliers or vendors. She advises, "See what they're doing and ask them questions, such as 'How could we get into a stronger, more coordinated relationship for the employees/patients we share?'"
- **Find out what you need.** Strong data and analytics are key to developing a health plan that is tailored to an

employee population. Without this information, administrators are flying blind. Thornhill recommends taking advantage of all available sources of health care data to understand how employees are using their health plans. These data will provide insights into the kind of care to prioritize for employees and the providers to include in your network to avoid disruptions in care.

Conclusion

Direct-to-employer contracting presents a paradigm shift in employer-provided health care. It can be a massive undertaking, but the payoffs are worth it, Thornhill says. "This was born out of companies feeling like insurance companies were making all the profits and they were handcuffed—like there was nothing else they could do—when, in fact, there are some options. It comes with a fair amount of investment and infrastructure. It's not free; it's not cheap; but in the long run, it's yielding results that are tangible."

References

FTI Consulting. 2022. "Direct-to-Employer Contracting Has Arrived." Published April 6. http://fticonsulting.com/insights/articles/direct-employer-contracting-arrived.

Mulvany, C. 2020. "Business Group on Health's Annual Survey: Large Employers Ready to Take the Reins on Healthcare Cost." Healthcare Financial Management Association. Published September 2. http://hfma.org/payment-reimbursement-and-managed-care/contracting/business-group-on-health-s-annual-survey-large-employers-ready.

The Economic Future of Health Care

With Eric Jordahl, Managing Director of Kaufman, Hall & Associates, LLC

Making predictions about the future is always a risky endeavor; making those predictions in an environment as unsettled as the one we face today compounds that risk. But if we assume the premise that the economic future of health care is itself unsettled, we can begin exploring scenarios that highlight potential effects on the financial stability of the US health care system and the probability that these effects will materialize.

Macroeconomic Risks

At the macroeconomic level, there is the question of the national debt. Earlier this year, vigorous debate took place around raising the federal government's debt ceiling, which had reached a staggering $31.4 trillion, almost double the $17 trillion level it reached in 2019. Much of this debate was, of course, political posturing; neither political party has shown much fiscal discipline in recent years. But a very serious—and unanswered—question underlies this debate: How much higher can our national debt go?

Some economists believe there is no technical limit on the debt, given the United States dollar's unique role as the reserve currency in the global economy. This role—and the resulting strong demand for the dollar by investors, including many of the world's central banks—enables the United States to keep borrowing at relatively low interest rates. This is true, so long as the global economy maintains its trust in the dollar. The risk of the dollar losing its place as the world's reserve currency is probably low, but the impact would be very high: history buffs can look to the series of currency crises and economic woes suffered by the United Kingdom through the 1960s and 1970s after the dollar took over the pound sterling as the reserve currency in the late 1950s (Harari 2017).

Health care is particularly exposed to this risk, or to the risk that one or both of the parties will rediscover their sense of fiscal discipline. Upward pressure on the national debt is driven primarily by the federal government's major entitlement programs: Social Security, Medicare, and Medicaid (which is shared with the states). No serious efforts at reducing the national debt can be made without taking on spending for these programs. And regardless of the debate over the national debt, Congress will have to make some decisions on these

programs relatively soon. Social Security is expected to run short of cash in about 10 years, and a key trust fund for Medicare is forecast to run out of funds by 2031. Unless changes are made to the 2023 Medicare program, this would result in an approximate 11 percent reduction in payments to health care providers (Horsley 2023). The alternative to payment reductions is a restructuring of Medicare benefits—which means touching a third rail in US politics—or increased funding for the program, which would likely require some new form of taxes.

The risk of payment cuts to Medicaid and, especially, Medicare is intensified by hospitals' and health systems' growing exposure to these programs. Many health care organizations already receive more than half of their payments from Medicare and Medicaid. As the population ages and the need for higher-acuity services increases, federal spending on Medicare alone is projected to rise from 10.1 percent of the 2021 federal budget to 17.8 percent of the 2032 federal budget, increasing from approximately $829 billion to more than $1.8 trillion (Cubanski and Neuman 2023). The number of Medicare beneficiaries is projected to grow from

About the Subject Matter Expert

Eric Jordahl is a managing director in Kaufman Hall's Treasury and Capital Markets practice. This practice focuses on helping health care organizations nationwide by providing treasury-related transactional, strategic, and management support across all financial assets and liabilities.

With a finance career spanning more than three decades, Eric has extensive experience working with client organizations of all sizes and levels of sophistication. His areas of expertise span all of the Treasury and Capital Markets product channels: credit and capital management, external financing (including derivative transactions), treasury operations, invested assets, treasury merger integration, and enterprise resource allocation. He also works with clients to assess and refine their organizational approach to the treasury function.

Prior to his time at Kaufman Hall, Eric spent 20 years in investment banking, advising a variety of health care organizations on transactions involving virtually every major asset class.

approximately 60 million in 2021 to more than 80 million in 2030: a 33 percent increase (Keisler-Starkey and Bunch 2022; Medicare Payment Advisory Commission 2015). By contrast, the number of individuals below age 65 with employer-sponsored insurance will barely budge, growing from 151 million in 2021 to 155 million in 2030: less than a 3 percent increase (Congressional Budget Office [CBO] 2020). The reality of this shift in payer mix is already understood by respondents to the 2023 *Futurescan* survey. Almost two-thirds indicated either that they had already seen a significant decrease in average reimbursement from commercial payers or that they expected to see a decrease by 2029.

The federal government's entanglement in health care expenditures extends well beyond government payment programs, however. The government also subsidizes significant portions of commercial health insurance expenditures. These subsidies include the exclusion of employer-paid premiums from employees' taxable income; subsidies of individual plans purchased on the state-level exchanges created by the Affordable Care Act; and tax deductions of health insurance premiums by many self-employed individuals. The government thus has an interest not only in keeping Medicare and Medicaid expenditures under control but also in controlling the costs of commercial health insurance. In the CBO's estimation, only price caps could potentially produce significant premium price reductions in commercial health plans and thus decrease the amount of subsidies the federal government pays (CBO 2022).

The crux of the problem for the economic future of hospitals and health systems is this: the federal government's involvement in the US health care system is vast and still growing, and there are pressures from many sides for the government to reduce the costs of its involvement. The risks presented by this involvement are similarly vast, even though they may today seem like distant storm clouds that may or may not strike with their full potential impact.

Industry-Specific Risks

Hospitals and health systems face another set of risks specific to the health care industry, most notably staffing issues (particularly with respect to the clinical workforce) and the disruption of care delivery models. While the risks presented at the macroeconomic level may be distant, they are still present and shaping the economic future of health care today.

Staffing shortages. The COVID-19 pandemic accelerated clinical workforce shortages that were predicted before the pandemic began. Over the course of 2021, the second year of the pandemic, the total supply of registered nurses (RNs) dropped by 100,000, "a far greater drop than ever observed over the past four decades" (Auerbach et al. 2022). Especially troubling was the fact that this decline was most concentrated in the population of RNs under the age of 35, almost entirely because of a reduction in hospital-employed nurses. With the average age of an RN now at 52 according to data from the American Association of Colleges of Nursing (AACN), the need to replenish the talent pipeline is urgent. But the AACN also reports that in 2021, US nursing schools turned away almost 92,000 qualified applications for baccalaureate and graduate nursing programs because of an insufficient number of faculty,

clinical sites, classroom space, and clinical preceptors, as well as budget constraints (AACN 2022).

Similar shortages are anticipated in the physician workforce. A 2021 report from the American Association of Medical Colleges projects a shortage of 17,800 to 48,000 primary care physicians and 21,000 to 77,000 non-primary care specialists by 2034 (IHS Markit 2021). Again, this problem is compounded by an aging physician workforce: according to the report, two of every five currently active physicians will be 65 or older within the next decade.

These shortages will have many effects on care delivery, as well as two primary economic impacts. First, as already witnessed during the pandemic, is the impact of demand exceeding supply, which manifests in the wage inflation that is necessary to recruit and retain clinical professionals. Kaufman Hall *National Hospital Flash Report* data indicate that hospital labor expenses are running almost 20 percent above pre-pandemic levels (Swanson 2023). Utilization of expensive contract labor has stabilized, but wages for full-time employees have settled at a significantly higher level. This is likely to be a permanent reset that results in a long-term increase in operating expenses.

The second impact is on revenues. Staffing shortages mean that hospitals and health systems may not be able to operate at full capacity. In a Kaufman Hall *State of Healthcare Performance Improvement* report (2022), for example, 66 percent of survey respondents said they had run their facilities at less than full capacity because of staffing shortages.

There are no quick fixes to staffing shortages. It takes time and resources to expand the educational programs that form the talent pipeline for new clinical professionals. And while technological advances, including artificial intelligence, may be able to alleviate shortages for certain functions (e.g., imaging and diagnostics), that too will take time and will not be a panacea for an industry that will have a significant human component for the foreseeable future.

Disruption of care delivery models.
Technological advances have already had a profound impact on care delivery models, as less invasive surgical procedures and shorter recovery times have enabled a growing number of procedures to move to outpatient and even home-based settings. Other services—including primary care and certain specialties such as radiology, psychiatry, dermatology, neurology, endocrinology, and rheumatology—are being successfully delivered using telemedicine. As the number of procedures on the "inpatient only" list shrinks, the competition faced by hospitals and health systems grows, as does downward pressure on revenue for these procedures.

In many markets, hospitals and health systems are already facing stiff competition from ambulatory surgery centers, often backed by private equity funding. National health plans also are pursuing a vertical integration strategy focused on acquisition of or affiliation with primary and multispecialty medical groups; UnitedHealth Group's Optum division now has the largest network of employed or aligned physicians in the United States (Emerson 2023). These organizations both compete directly against hospitals and health systems for business in key service lines (e.g., orthopedics, ophthalmology, cardiology,

oncology) and also seek, through value- and risk-based contracting arrangements, to reduce the need for acute care services. Already, almost 7 of 10 respondents to the SHSMD *Futurescan* survey say that a 15 percent or greater loss of their current total outpatient revenue to nontraditional health care disruptors either has already happened or is somewhat or very likely to happen by 2029.

Again, the economic effects on hospitals and health systems are two-pronged. First is the impact on volumes, as consumers gravitate toward care in more convenient, and often lower-cost, outpatient settings. Second is the impact on payments. As procedures move to outpatient settings, both commercial and governmental payers will push for site-neutral payment policies, eliminating hospital outpatient department (HOPD) rates and paying the same amount for a service or procedure regardless of the site of care (Samaris and Kinn 2021).

Some health systems may be able to mitigate the impact of these disruptive forces by reducing excess hospital capacity and the associated fixed costs; others, especially those in growing markets, may be able to replace services that move to outpatient or digital settings with high-demand inpatient services. But most health systems will have to make a decision on timing, determining

whether it is better to wait for volume and payment shifts or to take a near-term revenue loss to establish themselves as competitive, low-cost alternatives in their respective markets. Much will depend on the competitive landscape, opportunities for value-based contracting, and opportunities for partnerships or joint ventures with independent physician groups or other providers.

Key Takeaways
Not-for-profit hospitals and health systems face an array of macroeconomic and industry-specific economic risks in the coming years. Health care executives should be particularly attuned to the following risks:

- The federal government's involvement in the US health care system is vast and still growing, and there are pressures from many sides for the government to reduce the costs of its involvement. Risks include significant payment reductions in Medicare and Medicaid, as well as price caps for hospital and physician services to reduce the subsidies the government pays for commercial health plans.
- Staffing shortages in the clinical workforce are expected to persist and perhaps intensify. Economic risks include continued upward pressure on wages and negative impacts on revenue if hospitals and health

FUTURESCAN SURVEY RESULTS
Economics

Health care executives from across the nation were asked how likely it is that the following will happen in their hospital or health system by 2029.

By 2029, the average reimbursement our hospital or health system receives from commercial payers per patient will decrease by at least 10 percent.

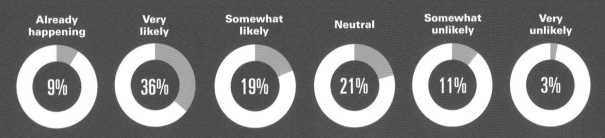

Already happening	Very likely	Somewhat likely	Neutral	Somewhat unlikely	Very unlikely
9%	36%	19%	21%	11%	3%

By 2029, more than 15 percent of current total outpatient revenue at our hospital or health system will be lost to nontraditional health care disruptors/competitors (e.g., physician-owned or for-profit/private-equity-backed ambulatory surgery centers, retail clinics, digital health companies, health plan–owned clinics).

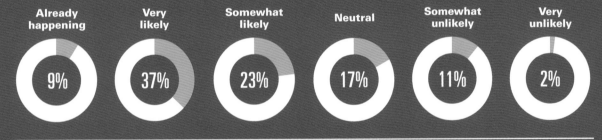

Already happening	Very likely	Somewhat likely	Neutral	Somewhat unlikely	Very unlikely
9%	37%	23%	17%	11%	2%

systems are unable to run at full capacity because of staffing shortages.

- Technological advances in care delivery have enabled significant growth in the amount of competition faced by hospitals and health systems as health care services and procedures continue to migrate from inpatient settings. Volumes for these services and procedures are at risk as consumers gravitate toward more convenient, lower-cost settings. In addition, payers—both commercial and governmental—will push for site-neutral payment policies, eliminating HOPD rates and paying the same amount for a service or procedure regardless of the site of care.

Conclusion: Repositioning Resources for a Structural Makeover

It seems increasingly likely that hospitals and health systems will require a structural makeover to align with health care's new economic realities. If that is the case, an organization's balance sheet will be the essential bridge between the present and a future, restructured health care sector. Given the many risks that hospitals and health systems face and the degree of uncertainty around some of the most significant risks, the journey will require careful planning about how to size, position, and deploy liquidity, leverage, and investments.

The central focus will be on how to reposition operations. But if organic cash generation remains anemic, the gap will be filled either by weakening the balance sheet (drawing down reserves, adding leverage, or adopting more aggressive asset allocation) or by partnering with organizations that have the necessary resources. Organizations reach the point of greatest enterprise risk when the scale of operating challenges outstrips the amount of balance sheet resources. Missteps are manageable when the imbalance is the product of rapid growth but not when it is the result of diminishing resources. If the core imperative is to remake operations, the co-equal imperative is to *continuously* reposition the balance sheet to carry your organization toward whatever defines future success.

References

American Association of Colleges of Nursing. 2022. "Fact Sheet: Nursing Shortage." Updated October. http://aacnnursing .org/Portals/0/PDFs/Fact-Sheets/Nursing-Shortage-Factsheet.pdf.

Auerbach, D., P. Buerhaus, K. Donelon, and D. Staiger. 2022. "A Worrisome Drop in the Number of Young Nurses." *Health Affairs*. Published April 13. http://healthaffairs.org/content/forefront/worrisome-drop-number-young-nurses.

Congressional Budget Office. 2022. "Policy Approaches to Reduce What Commercial Insurers Pay for Hospitals' and Physicians' Services." Published September 29. http://cbo.gov/publication/58222.

———. 2020. "Federal Subsidies for Health Insurance Coverage for People Under 65: 2020 to 2030." Published September 29. http://cbo.gov/publication/56571.

Cubanski, J., and T. Neuman. 2023. "What to Know About Medicare Spending and Financing." Kaiser Family Foundation. Published January 19. https://www.kff.org/medicare/issue-brief/what-to-know-about-medicare-spending-and-financing.

Emerson, J. 2023. "Meet America's Largest Employer of Physicians: UnitedHealth Group." *Becker's Payer Issues*. Updated February 16. http://beckerspayer.com/payer/meet-americas-largest-employer-of-physicians-unitedhealth-group.html.

Harari, D. 2017. "'Pound in Your Pocket' Devaluation: 50 Years On." UK Parliament, House of Commons Library. Published November 17. https://commonslibrary.parliament.uk/pound-in-your-pocket-devaluation-50-years-on.

Horsley, S. 2023. "Social Security Is Now Expected to Run Short of Cash by 2033." NPR. Published March 31. https://www .npr.org/2023/03/31/1167378958/social-security-medicare-entitlement-programs-budget.

IHS Markit. 2021. "The Complexities of Physician Supply and Demand: Projections from 2019 to 2034." Prepared for the Association of American Medical Colleges. Published June. https://www.aamc.org/media/54681/download?attachment.

Kaufman Hall. 2022. "2022 State of Healthcare Performance Improvement: Mounting Pressures Pose New Challenges." Published October 10. http://kaufmanhall.com/sites/default/files/2022-10/2022-State-Healthcare-Performance -Improvement.pdf.

Keisler-Starkey, K., and L. N. Bunch. 2022. "Health Insurance Coverage in the United States: 2021." US Census Bureau. Published September 13. http://census.gov/library/publications/2022/demo/p60-278.html.

Medicare Payment Advisory Commission. 2015. "Medicare Payment Advisory Commission Releases Report on Medicare and the Health Care Delivery System." Published June 15. http://medpac.gov/wp-content/uploads/import_data/scrape _files/docs/default-source/press-releases/medpac-releases-june-2015-report-on-medicare-and-the-health-care-delivery -system.pdf.

Samaris, D., and J. Kinn. 2021. "Responding to the Risk of Site-Neutral Payments." Kaufman Hall. Published September 16. http://kaufmanhall.com/insights/responding-risk-site-neutral-payments.

Swanson, E. 2023. "National Hospital Flash Report: July 2023." Kaufman Hall. Published July 28. http://kaufmanhall.com /sites/default/files/2023-07/KH-NHFR_2023-07.pdf.

The Intersection of Social Determinants of Health, Innovation, Technology, and a Growing Medicaid Population

with Kameron Matthews, MD, JD, FAAFP, Chief Health Officer, Cityblock Health

Nearly 150 million Americans rely on federal health care benefits through Medicare, Medicaid, and the State Children's Health Insurance Program. Over the next five years, hospitals and health systems can expect to see a dramatic increase in the number of patients who have Medicaid as their primary payment source and the number of patients who are dual-eligible for both Medicare and Medicaid.

Kameron Matthews, MD, JD, FAAFP, chief health officer of Cityblock Health, recommends that hospitals and health systems adopt the concept of "whole-person care" to adequately respond to these reimbursement and population trends because the patients who are involved face entrenched inequities in care and have been marginalized historically.

Caring for the health of these individuals means addressing social and economic factors, such as a person's financial stability, the home and neighborhood in which they live, their access to a quality education and affordable health care, and their connection to community support, Matthews says. According to the Robert Wood Johnson Foundation (RWJF), social determinants of health drive as much as 80 percent of health outcomes, and social factors account for more than one-third of all deaths: more than smoking and obesity combined (RWJF 2019). The RWJF website, Congressional Districts and Health: What Can Be Measured?, offers a health snapshot of all 435 congressional districts, plus Washington, DC (RWJF 2023).

"'Stovepipe' solutions, focused specifically on a single disease state or a single social determinant of health, may be able to meet specific quality

About the Subject Matter Expert

Kameron Matthews, MD, JD, FAAFP, is the chief health officer of Cityblock Health, a health care provider for Medicaid, dually eligible, and lower-income Medicare beneficiaries that partners with community-based organizations and health plans to deliver medical care, behavioral health care, and social services virtually, in homes and in community-based clinics. Prior to joining Cityblock, Matthews worked as a staff physician at Cook County Jail and with Erie Family Health Center in Chicago. She also served as the chief medical officer of Mile Square Health Center at the University of Illinois Hospital and Health Sciences System. Later, Matthews joined the Veterans Health Administration, serving as assistant undersecretary for health for community care, chief medical officer, and assistant undersecretary for health for clinical services. Matthews was the 2018–2020 National Academy of Medicine–American Board of Family Medicine James C. Puffer Fellow and in 2020 was elected to the National Academy of Medicine.

outcomes, but we won't be able to address the *health* of this population if we don't work from a holistic standpoint," Matthews explains, noting that health systems tend to focus on specialty care because that is where fee-for-service reimbursement is concentrated. "The leading strategy that CEOs need to deploy is prioritization and expansion of primary care services. Primary care earns trust. If leadership fails to do that, this population will continue to mistrust health systems and to go to the emergency department for avoidable situations."

According to the most recent *Futurescan* survey, more than half of responding health care leaders said it was somewhat or very likely that by 2029 their hospital or health system would experience at least a 20 percent increase in the demand for care from patients with Medicaid as their primary payment source. Nearly half of the respondents said they expect to see a 20 percent drop in per-patient Medicaid reimbursements over the same period.

Deploying Technology More Effectively for Medicaid Populations

Technology and digital tools must be more effectively deployed to improve hospitals' ability to meet the needs of these at-risk populations, allowing health systems to be as agnostic as possible toward a patient's form of insurance coverage. In her leadership role at the Department of Veterans Affairs (VA), Matthews observed the lack of visibility between payor systems.

"I had veterans enrolled in three different payors—Tricare, VA Community Care, and Medicare—and we had no visibility into their other eligibilities," she recalls. "They had to pick and choose. They'd come to us for pharmacy because we had the best prices, to Tricare because it had the best selection, and to Medicare for other reasons. That's just mind-boggling. Being segmented and siloed based on what insurance plan a patient is enrolled in is not patient centered at all. This is one example that's specific to my time working with veterans, but this kind of fragmentation

is happening across the health care system."

According to Matthews, health systems should invest in technology that enables them to manage the two programs of dually eligible patients and their associated administrative burdens in ways that do not force those burdens onto the patient or the clinical care teams. Ideally, electronic health records should automatically allow providers to merge multiple sets of services and coverage.

"It's time to think about your technology stack as more than just billing and the electronic health record; it has to be focused on coordination," Matthews argues. "These solutions will have to come from someone in the innovation space. There are many potential partners in the digital world. Isn't it worth it to get us to a health care system that is person centered and can also reduce the burnout that is overwhelming our provider workforce?"

To provide true value-based care, Matthews adds, the tools for care teams should be adapted to reflect longitudinal and whole-person care across a person's life span, as opposed to the episodic, "point in time" documentation seen in most current electronic health records and other IT systems used in hospitals.

"If the clinician is forced to look at their data in acute bundles and not in whole experiences and data sets over time, we're never going to change how

we deliver care to be more holistic," she says. Matthews is encouraged by the fact that the Office of the National Coordinator for Health Information Technology is releasing more technological requirements for interoperability and focus on social determinants of health.

Innovative Solutions for Addressing the Primary Care Needs of the Growing Medicaid Population

At Cityblock, Matthews leads efforts to transform primary care for vulnerable populations, such as facilitated primary care and an integrated psychiatry and clinical pharmacy program.

"The average person on Medicaid has had difficulty, if not outright trauma, in accessing the health care system," she explains. "It behooves us to first earn their trust and engage with them, which means we need to go to them and provide services in a way that is easiest for them. Setting up offices and saying, 'Come see us' is not sufficient. That is why, at Cityblock Health, we have these multiple different opportunities for our members to access care—meeting them in the community, in their homes— when they are willing to."

Cityblock's integrated-care teams consist of a community health partner (who has a similar background and training as a community health worker), a nurse care manager, a nurse

FUTURESCAN SURVEY RESULTS
Medicaid

Health care executives from across the nation were asked how likely it is that the following will happen in their hospital or health system by 2029.

By 2029, we will see at least a 20 percent increase in the demand for care from patients who have Medicaid as their primary payment source at our hospital or health system.

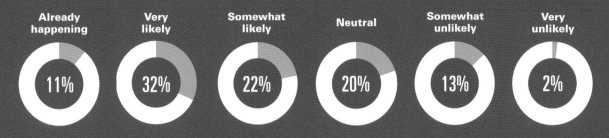

Already happening	Very likely	Somewhat likely	Neutral	Somewhat unlikely	Very unlikely
11%	32%	22%	20%	13%	2%

By 2029, we will see an average 20 percent decrease in the amount of reimbursement we receive from Medicaid per patient served by our hospital or health system.

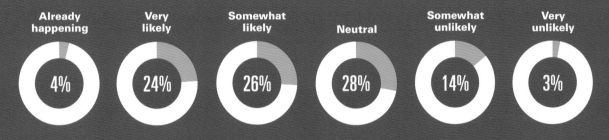

Already happening	Very likely	Somewhat likely	Neutral	Somewhat unlikely	Very unlikely
4%	24%	26%	28%	14%	3%

---

practitioner or physician primary care provider, a behavioral health therapist, and a psychiatrist. The community health partner is responsible for checking in with the patient via phone call or text message on an ongoing basis to understand their care plan progress and flag issues for the rest of the medical team as necessary.

Meanwhile, with facilitated primary care, a patient's visit takes place in their home but is not solely virtual. "We send a staff member into their home to look them in the eye, sit with them, observe their environment, and talk about their social needs," Matthews explains. "Then the staff member connects them with the primary care doctor for the virtual visit on an iPad or laptop. It's all about meeting people where they are. One of the travesties of our hospitals and academic medical centers is this concept of the ivory tower. Patients must come in to see us, and we expect them to figure out how to get transportation or park and how to traverse more than just the confusing physical space of these campuses. At Cityblock Health, we partner with hospitals and academic medical centers, but we will be by our members' sides when they need to go in and get their specialty services."

Cityblock's overarching goal is to create an interdisciplinary one-stop shop for patients, a single primary care team with the patient at the center. These proactive teams reach out to patients on a regular basis, seeking to address their social and medical needs through community partnerships with local food banks, transportation organizations, and housing initiatives. Mental and behavioral health is also critical for serving the needs of the growing Medicaid population. An analysis by the Kaiser Family Foundation found that 39 percent of Medicaid enrollees live with a mental-health or substance-abuse problem (Saunders and Rudowitz 2022).

Matthews points out that mental-health workers are often concentrated in geographical areas that are far from low-income communities or historically marginalized populations. "Mental-health professionals generally tend not to have a comfort level in treating Black and brown populations, and often lack an understanding of racialized trauma or larger concepts of trauma-informed care," she says.

Through its programming, Cityblock purposely focuses on patients with serious mental illness and substance-use disorders: people who experience significant care gaps within Medicaid.

"We actively invite those patients to join our primary care practices," Matthews explains. "We have full psychiatric support in the ambulatory environment, as well as addiction medicine, and consider those staff members part of our primary care team without differentiating between physical health and mental health and social needs. We're also piloting an advanced behavioral health program that focuses on our highest-risk membership, aimed at increasing their engagement, decreasing hospitalizations and emergency department visits, increasing outpatient treatment, and initiating long-acting medication-assisted therapy for substance use. In a pilot cohort, we saw a 15 percent decrease in emergency department visits in DC for members engaged in our Advanced Behavioral Health program."

State Variability Is a Challenge to Innovation and Flexibility in Medicaid

At the state level, wide variability in how programs are administered and implemented poses obstacles to improving Medicaid programs and promoting innovation and flexibility for safety-net hospitals. The goal must be to better deliver on the mission of these hospitals and address social determinants of health, according to Matthews. As of spring 2023, 10 states still refuse the opportunity offered by the Affordable Care Act to expand Medicaid to hundreds of thousands of additional low-income Americans, she says.

In addition, although Medicaid is federally coordinated, eligibility and enrollment criteria are managed by the states. In many states, individuals must renew their Medicaid coverage every 12 months, but a change in income or employment or a lack of support with renewal can lead to coverage disruption that is often associated with delays in the preventive health care that could improve their outcomes. With the end of the COVID-19 public health emergency (PHE), Medicaid beneficiaries who have not had their coverage renewed during the PHE will need to go through the redetermination process to maintain coverage. Although states must complete these redeterminations in compliance with Medicaid and Constitutional due process, millions of people could lose coverage.

"It is unacceptable that, based on where you live, you have a difference in the services that are available to you through Medicaid and correspondingly in your outcomes," Matthews says. "There are innovative Medicaid programs at the population level in some states, and they are important, but their benefits will be limited unless there's some effort to make them available for all beneficiaries within Medicaid. That is deprioritized because these people are deprioritized. The same doctor is paid less for the same care, because this program is valued less and these people are seen as less worthy of tax dollars. Therefore, hospitals and health systems can act accordingly and deny service or provide less coordinated services to their Medicaid patients as opposed to their commercial and Medicare patients."

Federal legislation such as the Supporting States in Integrating Care Act, the Advancing Integration in Medicare and Medicaid Act, and the Comprehensive Care for Dual Eligible Individuals Act aim to improve integrated care for dually eligible individuals, but Matthews notes that none of them addresses the larger issue about the lack of Medicaid standardization between the states.

"It is quite difficult operationally to integrate care between Medicare and Medicaid if there isn't some kind of consistency about how the states do it," she notes. "Medicare won't be able to build out real efficiencies if interactions with the states aren't streamlined in some way. States like California and Massachusetts will continue to be advanced in improving integrated care, but we will still have many states lagging behind, particularly the 10 that did not expand Medicaid."

Incentivizing Hospitals to Pursue Health Equity Goals for Harder-to-Serve Patients

Unfortunately, according to Matthews, value-based care models implemented by the federal government, such as the pilot Merit-Based Incentive Payment System, are designed to get health systems to focus on uncoordinated outcomes that do not promote goals of health equity.

"Our model allows us to focus on improving the quality of care and the quality of outcomes and to decrease the cost of care, as opposed to the fee-for-service model, which is typically more process based," she says. "Unfortunately, a lot of federal programs, in seeking to drive certain activity, are inordinately focused on process and checklists. Even with care management, which is an important part of this holistic, whole-person care that Cityblock is providing in the value-based care, we still see emphasis on some administrative tasks rather than the outcomes we achieve for individual members."

Key Takeaways

To meet the challenges posed by Medicaid expansion, Matthews advises health systems to take the following measures:

- **Deploy technology and digital tools to improve their ability to meet the needs of at-risk populations.** These tools effectively allow health systems to be as "agnostic as possible toward a patient's form of insurance coverage" and to avoid "siloing" patients based on insurance plans, given the regular attrition and changing landscape of coverage options. Technology can assist systems in managing the administrative burdens associated with dually eligible patients without passing these challenges on to them.

- **Use innovative solutions to engage patients and build trust.** At Cityblock, Matthews and her colleagues have developed integrated-care teams that consist of community health partners, nurse care managers, nurse practitioners or primary care providers, behavioral health therapists, and psychiatrists. The primary goal is to create an interdisciplinary one-stop shop for patients. However, these proactive teams also reach out to patients on a regular basis, seeking to address their social and medical needs through community partnerships with local food banks, transportation organizations, and housing initiatives.

- **Collection of more comprehensive and consistent data around race, ethnicity, gender identity, and sexual orientation is also essential to mapping out evidence-based solutions and interventions around health inequities.** "We can't address the inequities that are occurring without measuring them, and we can't incentivize payors, health systems, and practices to address health equity if they aren't being held to some requirement to measure where

the inequities are in the first place," Matthews notes.

Conclusion

Despite the challenges inherent in the current Medicaid environment, Matthews remains enthusiastic about newer pilot programs—such as initiatives in several states by the Centers for Medicare & Medicaid Services that involve funding for different social care services—that could finally put the focus in the right places, including social determinants of health that often make patients who have been marginalized, minoritized, or traumatized more difficult to treat.

"The Biden administration's focus on reimbursing for an array of services that address social determinants of health is an exciting step," Matthews says. "It's just a pilot in four states now, but I'm optimistic about it. This is an approach that can truly allow these hospitals to build out additional services so they can take care of the whole person. We know the piecemeal traditional medicine approach to these patients isn't working. Hospitals must be able to treat the whole patient, and the only way to do that is to reimburse for holistic care, including social needs like food, housing, and transportation."

References

Robert Wood Johnson Foundation (RWJF). 2023. "Congressional Districts and Health: What Can Be Measured?" Published January 25. http://rwjf.org/en/insights/our-research/2023/01/congressional-districts-and-health--what-can-be-measured-.html.

———. 2019. "Medicaid's Role in Addressing Social Determinants of Health." Published February 1. http://rwjf.org/en/insights/our-research/2019/02/medicaid-s-role-in-addressing-social-determinants-of-health.html.

Saunders, H., and R. Rudowitz. 2022. "Demographics and Health Insurance Coverage of Nonelderly Adults with Mental Illness and Substance Use Disorders in 2020." Published June 6. http://kff.org/medicaid/issue-brief/demographics-and-health-insurance-coverage-of-nonelderly-adults-with-mental-illness-and-substance-use-disorders-in-2020.

Responsible Innovation and the Digital Transformation of Health Care

with Stephen Klasko, MD, MBA, Executive-in-Residence at General Catalyst

Health care is undergoing a seismic shift as technological innovations continue to reshape the landscape. From the explosive growth of telemedicine during the COVID-19 pandemic to new digital solutions that are bridging the gaps between providers and patients, there is little doubt that technology is transforming health care delivery. This transformation is finally addressing health equity issues, especially in traditionally underserved communities. Over the next five years, hospitals and health care systems that invest in and become involved with "responsible innovation" through new and creative partnerships will be the drivers of change and supporters of health equity.

However, health-system leaders must think outside the traditional box to bring innovations to the populations that need them most. The next five years promise to be transformative for health care and hospital systems, with further integration of digital technologies and predictive analytics and partnerships with former competitors and venture capital firms that will make innovation more likely. So how can health systems fund and become part of these digital innovations that will drive meaningful change?

Venture Capital and the Future of Transformation in Health Care

The role of venture capital will continue to grow as health systems embrace technology to improve operations and bring clinical care into the communities. Stephen Klasko, MD, MBA, former president and CEO of Thomas Jefferson University and Jefferson Health in Philadelphia, and executive-in-residence of venture capital firm General Catalyst, sees venture capital's role in driving health care transformation as more focused on responsible innovation,

Stephen Klasko, MD, MBA, is the former president and CEO of Thomas Jefferson University and Jefferson Health in Philadelphia and currently serves as executive-in-residence of General Catalyst, a leading venture capital firm dedicated to building companies that are changing the status quo through responsible innovation. Klasko is a transformative leader and an advocate for a revolution in the health care system in the United States. Passionate about using technology and innovation to eliminate health disparities and promote health assurance, he regularly speaks and writes about his vision for reconstructing the US health system by bridging traditional academic centers and hospital systems with entrepreneurs and innovators.

During Klasko's tenure at Jefferson, his work included reducing health inequity through payor–provider alignment, diversification of the system's portfolio, and partnerships with venture capital firms that were committed to responsible innovation. He believes that these areas are what today's health care leaders must focus on to keep up with the digital revolution in health care that will continue over the next five years and beyond.

which he says is critical to the health care environment. Klasko's current role is to look at areas where "we can turn population health, social determinants of health, predictive analytics, and health equity from philosophy and academics—where they are today—to the mainstream of clinical care and payment models."

Forward-thinking leaders look at how new technologies will affect the social determinants of health and make these innovations a part of their mission and vision. In the past, these digital trans-formations were viewed as disruptive in the same manner that ride-sharing was disruptive to taxi companies. The traditional health care ecosystem was "stuck in its lanes," Klasko says. Hospitals needed more sick people to fill their beds, payors needed to decrease the medical loss ratio, and venture capital companies created solutions that did not always move the needle. "More recently, venture capital firms like General Catalyst are starting to look at social issues and proacting, as opposed to reacting, to them," he adds.

Cityblock Health, one of the first companies in General Catalyst's health assurance portfolio, is an example of how the marriage between venture capital and community health services provides care to underserved groups. Launched in New York City to deliver personalized primary and behavioral health care and social services to people on Medicaid and to lower-income Medicare beneficiaries, Cityblock Health focuses on keeping people out of the hospital and sharing the savings with health care systems. The company moved care into communities through a network of clinics and developed in-home and virtual care options as well as custom care delivery technology.

The *Futurescan* survey found broad agreement among hospital CEOs and strategy leaders that successful health sys-tems will invest in a development fund to help reduce health care disparities and keep patients from needing in-hospital care. About 22 percent of all respondents are already doing this, and nearly half predict that it is somewhat or very likely that they will do so in the coming years.

Promoting Responsible Innovation

Venture capital firms are looking to identify areas where health care is out of reach and to partner with health companies like Cityblock Health to fill in the gaps. This trend—what General Catalyst calls "responsible innovation"—is likely to continue for the foreseeable future.

"Responsible innovation means that we must look at bringing these innova-tions to the populations who need them the most," Klasko explains. "Currently, improving access to health care means getting more sick people into the hos-pitals, but what if we turn the focus to creating health assurance, taking health care to the underserved communities and focusing on keeping people away from the high-fixed-cost hospitals?"

Klasko suggests that health leaders should think about collaborating with companies that are providing services to nontraditional, overlooked, and under-served patient populations. How can hospital systems partner with emerging companies that are filling a critical need in underserved communities, and how can they expand the portfolio of strate-gic partners for health equity?

He predicts that investments in dig-ital innovations and in companies that will care for marginalized communities will continue to grow over the next five years. Venture capital firms may expand their portfolios with this mission in

mind. For example, General Catalyst added Equip Health—which focuses on providing virtual, evidence-based care and treatment for individuals with eating disorders so they can recover at home—to its health assurance portfo-lio. Another addition was Homeward Health, whose mission is to remove barriers to health care for people living in rural communities through the use of various technologies, including tele-medicine, remote monitoring, mobile clinics, and partnerships with commu-nity health resources.

The *Futurescan* survey again reflected broad agreement with this prediction. Over 27 percent of respondents are already collaborating with others to address health equity issues, and half of all respondents predict this is somewhat or very likely in the future.

Thinking More Entrepreneurially

Klasko believes that one should think boldly to keep moving health care for-ward. It will require a "radical" mindset, he says—radical collaboration, radical communication, and radical concen-tration on reducing health disparities. With the venture capital space turning increasingly to socially relevant compa-nies that provide digital innovations and solutions to help level the playing field in health care delivery, Klasko recom-mends that leaders consider strategic collaborations with venture capital and

FUTURESCAN SURVEY RESULTS
Responsible Innovation

Health care executives from across the nation were asked how likely it is that the following will happen in their hospital or health system by 2029.

By 2029, our hospital or health system will have invested in or cocreated a development fund to reduce health inequities and keep care out of the hospitals (e.g., by addressing social determinants of health and other health-related disparities).

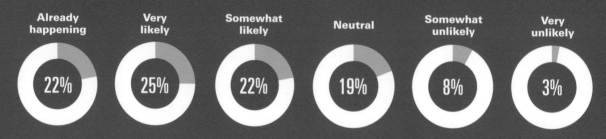

Already happening	Very likely	Somewhat likely	Neutral	Somewhat unlikely	Very unlikely
22%	25%	22%	19%	8%	3%

By 2029, our hospital or health system will form joint collaboratives for health equity solutions across regional/geographic areas with various entities to solve health equity issues.

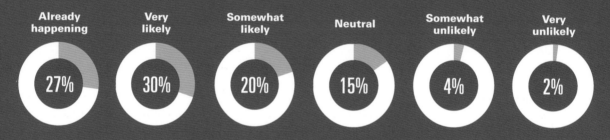

Already happening	Very likely	Somewhat likely	Neutral	Somewhat unlikely	Very unlikely
27%	30%	20%	15%	4%	2%

other health partners over the next five years.

"Think more entrepreneurially about partnering with venture capital firms," he advises. "At Jefferson, we worked with the people who believed in responsible innovation and the things we were doing around population health and social determinants."

Tendo, a health care software company, provides an example of a partnership between a health system, a digital technology provider, and a venture capital firm that resulted in a solution that addresses population health, access to care, and health equity. In March 2021, Jefferson Health and General Catalyst teamed up with Tendo to launch an engagement platform that connects patients, clinicians, and caregivers throughout the care cycle. Even in these days of electronic health records and connected data, patient health information and medical records still tend to be disconnected, depending on where and when patients receive care. Tendo's digital solution helped Jefferson Health tie together the patient journey into one application, providing a more consumer-friendly experience.

"Tendo came in and listened to the problems we were experiencing at Jefferson (such as reaching patients within our communities), looked at the resources available, and worked with General Catalyst to develop the digital solution we needed," Klasko notes. "They shared our vision of better access and health care with no address."

It is this type of creative partnership, or what Klasko calls "radical collaboration," that health care leaders need to engage in to develop the transformations that focus on health equity over the next five years. "Combining the entrepreneurial, bold spirit of Tendo with the mission-driven, sometimes risk-averse health system perspective allowed us to be measured on how to innovate," he says. "Innovation happens slowly and steadily. Ideally, it is focused at first and then scales loudly."

Klasko cautions that health care leaders and venture capital firms alike must be careful to ensure that the latest innovations do not just make the wealthy healthier: "At Jefferson, we partnered with companies throughout the ecosphere that were looking at getting care out to people no matter what their social and financial situation was. As we talk about the digital transformation of health care, it's incredibly important that leaders look at how these new technologies will affect the social determinants."

Radical Collaboration and Payor–Provider Alignment

So how do hospitals and health care systems afford this transformation and the innovations that are rapidly reshaping health care delivery? Klasko recommends focusing on:

- diversifying a health system's portfolio through innovation,
- creating strategic partnerships and collaborating with health systems and hospitals that were once considered the competition, and
- aligning payors and providers.

"Payor–provider alignment and collaboration with the right strategic partners are keys to succeeding in health care's future. It's very hard to reduce health inequity if you don't have a percentage of premium model," he states.

Klasko did exactly this during his tenure at Jefferson Health, when the health system took an ownership stake in a health insurance plan to address health inequities, shifting away from traditional hospital-based models of care and toward more community-based and patient-centered approaches.

In November 2021, Jefferson Health acquired the remaining 50 percent stake in Health Partners Plans from the Temple University Health System,

making Jefferson the sole owner of the not-for-profit health maintenance organization. The acquisition enabled Jefferson to advance its value-based care model while reducing the costs of health care services, particularly to underserved patients and families in the greater Philadelphia region.

Health systems don't necessarily need to buy a health insurance company to align with payors, however. Creative partnerships will be required. Klasko points to the accountable care organization (ACO) created by Jefferson Health and Main Line Health as an example of payor–provider alignment.

"We got together with Main Line's leaders and asked, what if we took this ACO and its huge primary care base and looked at Medicare Shared Savings Plans and Medicare Advantage? So, we partnered with Humana as a co-owner of the ACO. Humana recognized the opportunity for this collaboration and partnership," he says.

Emphasizing that this type of radical collaboration isn't just for large health systems, Klasko also cites several smaller hospitals that banded together in New Jersey to create an ACO as another example of how health care leaders can create payor–provider alignment.

"What if we think about shifting health care from a sick-care model to a model where we collaborate and find the right partners to ensure the health of communities and people?" asks

Klasko. He emphasizes that health care CEOs must look at other hospitals and regional health systems not as competitors but as strategic partners.

Becoming Innovative Cocreators

According to Klasko, health care leaders should look at what is going to be obvious in five years and do it now. "The old math of inpatient and outpatient revenue and NIH [National Institutes of Health] funding [for academic centers] no longer works," he says. "Leaders must get involved in the new math of payor–provider alignment and diversifying their portfolios."

Hospital and health systems looking to diversify their portfolios will benefit from becoming co-developers of the innovations being used to deliver care and improve operations, since that not only improves their quality and delivery of health care but also creates an opportunity to earn equity in the technologies and solutions that are co-developed.

Klasko advises health care CEOs to work with their boards to identify ways to invest in and diversify their portfolios, especially in digital innovations. "If you believe enough in a digital technology to use it and to help a technology company develop it, then the chances are it is going to grow. If you have a percentage of this innovation, a $2 million investment can turn into a $10 million one," Klasko explains.

Alignment with Your Hospital's Mission

Klasko is passionate about ensuring that health systems and hospitals align their mission, vision, and values with technological innovation so that all stakeholders—the hospital, community, and workforce—understand the "why" and buy in to the goals.

"At Jefferson, we realized that our original mission—being the premier academic medical center in Philadelphia—didn't reflect the population's needs," Klasko notes. "Being the best wasn't helping the sickest, so we changed our mission to 'We Improve Lives.' The other part of this is tying incentives to improving people's lives, which is why 25 percent of my personal incentive as president of the university and CEO of the health system was tied to reducing health disparities and meeting our mission."

Klasko makes this point: "Don't just talk about health inequity—live it." He emphasizes that it is important not only to invest in innovations but also to participate in them. Health care leaders can ensure that innovations are developed responsibly and that equity is a major factor in incentives and the organization's mission, vision, and values.

Key Takeaways

Health care innovation and digital transformation are forging ahead, and health care leaders who can think outside the traditional ecosystem will lead the way into a new era of responsible innovation and equity in health care. Klasko offers three recommendations for health care executives to consider for adopting responsible innovation over the next five years.

- **Participate in radical collaboration and strategic partnerships**. "Your competition isn't the hospital across the street; these are your collaborators," Klasko says. "Get together around population health. Work with your hospital board so that the CEO payment structure mirrors your organization's mission and vision. Engage your workforce. Then you will be able to institute a digital transformation." He urges leaders to identify the issues that technology can help solve and to align with strategic partners who are making health care accessible to out-of-reach and underserved communities.
- **Diversify your portfolio through innovation, strategic partnerships, and philanthropy, and focus on payor–provider alignment.** "The traditional source of revenue—getting patients into beds—is not sustainable as health care continues to evolve. CEOs and boards must start to get creative and diversify." Klasko adds that payor–provider alignment and collaboration with the right strategic partners will "allow you to talk to payors at different levels about how to work together for more equitable care."
- **Think radically.** "Look at what's going to be hot in five years and then adopt those innovations today. Think about where digital technology can help you now and what innovations can be developed for the future," Klasko says. "Share in that innovation equity and growth to diversify your portfolio. Health care isn't going to progress under the traditional mindset of inching forward to avoid risk at all costs."

Klasko concludes that health care leaders should not "play to tie." He urges leaders, "Play to win. Health care CEOs and boards must be willing to be bold, think differently and take measured risks around health equity and responsible innovation."

Society for Health Care Strategy & Market Development

The Society for Health Care Strategy & Market Development (SHSMD), a professional membership group of the AHA, is the largest and most prominent voice for health care strategists. SHSMD serves strategists across diverse disciplines, providing essential knowledge, leading-edge tools and invaluable connections. SHSMD empowers members to overcome obstacles, foresee the future and drive change, towards the vision of a world with healthier people and communities achieved through bold, actionable and inclusive strategies. For more information about Futurescan, contact SHSMD at 312.422.3888 or shsmd@aha.org.

American College of Healthcare Executives/Health Administration Press

The American College of Healthcare Executives is an international professional society of more than 48,000 healthcare executives who lead hospitals, healthcare systems and other healthcare organizations. ACHE's mission is to advance its members and healthcare management excellence. ACHE offers its prestigious FACHE® credential, signifying board certification in healthcare management. ACHE's established network of 77 chapters provides access to networking, education and career development at the local level. In addition, ACHE is known for its magazine, *Healthcare Executive*, and its career development and public policy programs. Through such efforts, ACHE works toward its vision of being the preeminent professional society for leaders dedicated to improving health.

The Foundation of the American College of Healthcare Executives was established to further advance healthcare management excellence through education and research. The Foundation of ACHE is known for its educational programs—including the annual Congress on Healthcare Leadership, which draws more than 4,000 participants—and groundbreaking research. Its publishing division, Health Administration Press, is one of the largest publishers of books and journals on health services management, including textbooks for college and university courses. For more information, visit www.ache.org.

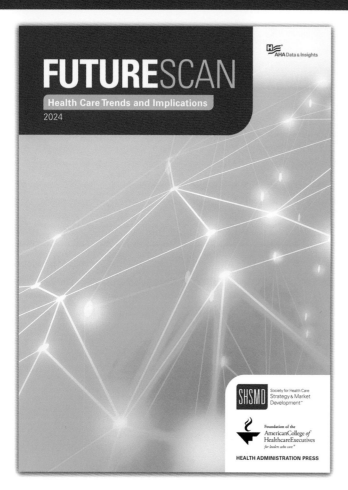